MARY ROSE'S

*1001 COUNTRY
GARDEN TIPS*

To VICKY
FROM Mum

MARY ROSE'S

1001 COUNTRY GARDEN TIPS

Published in the UK exclusively for

SELECTABOOK
Folly Road
Roundway
Devizes
Wiltshire
SN10 2HR

Produced by TAJ BOOKS
27 Ferndown Gardens
Cobham
Surrey
KT11 2BH

Email: info@tajbooks.com

Text © 2003 Mary Rose Quigg
Design and layout © 2003 TAJ BOOKS Ltd

ISBN 1-84406-009-8

Printed and bound in China

ONTENTS

❋ ❋ ❋ ❋ ❋

ACKNOWLEDGEMENTS

I would like to dedicate this book to my husband Joe as he is the real gardener around our house. My thanks to Karen, Arleen, Orla, Cathal and Brenda for their encouragement and support.

$\mathcal{I}$NTRODUCTION

*"There is a great pleasure in working in the soil,
apart from the ownership of it.
The man who has planted a garden feels that
he has done something for the good of the world"*

Gardening for some is a way of life, and for others is a nice hobby to keep them occupied. Regardless of the purpose of your garden this collection of valuable hints and tips should help to make day to day tasks more easily completed.

In this environmentally friendly age it is important to use natural products when appropriate and this is the theme throughout this book.

All aspects of gardening are covered from flowers and houseplants to planting shrubs, vegetables, herbs and trees. The garden pests and tools chapters give very useful tips while healthy gardening should assist in avoiding all those aches and pains. The poems and proverbs included always give me great delight and I hope they make the book more enjoyable.

I have had great pleasure in compiling this practical book from hints and tips that I have acquired over the years. I hope that there is something of interest for you in it and that you find it helpful, interesting and entertaining. Most of all let it be useful to you in the pursuit of a perfect garden.

MARY ROSE

*A swarm of bees in May
Is worth a load of hay;
A swarm of bees in June
Is worth a silver spoon;
A swarm of bees in July
Is not worth a fly.*

Say it With Flowers

I wandered lonely as a cloud
That floats on high o'er vales and hills,
When all at once I saw a crowd,
A host, of golden daffodils;
Beside the lake, beneath the trees,
Fluttering and dancing in the breeze.

Continuous as the stars that shine
And twinkle on the milky way,
They stretched in never-ending line
Along the margin of a bay:
Ten thousand saw I at a glance,
Tossing their heads in sprightly dance.
                    by William Wordsworth

LEGENDS & LORE

Some species of flowers are considered unlucky in many parts of the world, particularly when brought into the house.

Honeysuckle, if brought into the house brought bad luck in Wales but foretold a wedding in Somerset.

The wild foxglove is a fairy plant in folk-tradition. The Irish believe that foxgloves in the house are unlucky. It should never be taken aboard a ship. To pick the foxglove offends the fairies that live within the flowers and will bring bad luck, even death, to the picker and his family. Foxgloves are very poisonous.

In the west of England, if snowdrops are brought into the house before the first chickens are hatched, all the eggs will be addled.

In Surrey, to take the first primrose into the house meant sickness and sorrow.

In Norfolk, lilac was considered unlucky.

In the last century in England, a bunch of violets worn around the neck or in the lapel protected against drunkenness.

Red and white flowers in the same vase were unlucky, and even today some nurses will not have these flowers in the same vase on a ward.

Blue and orange flowers were welcome in homes and hospitals as these colours calm the nerves.

The name iris is the Greek word for the rainbow. They were planted on women's graves.

Lavender has a long reputation as an anaphrodisiac.

The rose is known as the queen of flowers. The white rose represents simplicity or happy love, the white rose is for innocence and purity, the yellow rose means perfect achievement and sometimes jealousy and the red rose signifies passion and sensual desire or shame and occasionally blood and sacrifice.

"A garden is a friend you can visit any time."

CUT FLOWERS

Pick garden flowers in the cool of the morning or in the evening. If it has been raining and the flowers are wet, shake them gently to remove the excess water.

Choose half-open blooms or buds with a little colour showing. If picked too tightly in bud, they may never open. This is especially true of tulips and roses.

The green pointed sepals around the base of the rose should be starting to turn downwards. Irises and daffodils should be half opened.

Gladioli should be picked when the bottom three or four florets are open and the top florets are still in bud.

Carnations, dahlias, marigolds, hydrangeas, camellias, and chrysanthemums should be picked when they are fully opened.

Take the bucket of warm water into the garden when cutting flowers. Use a sharp pair of secateurs and cut the flower stems at an angle - a slanted cut allows a better intake of water.

Remove all foliage from the lower portion of the stems standing under the water line as foliage left on stems below the water line will rot and pollute the water. Place the flowers immediately in the water.

Never overcrowd flowers. Allow enough air to circulate between each flower. Too many flowers crowded together in a bucket may cause the petals to become squashed and bruised. Place the bucket in a cool dark place and allow the flowers to have a long drink before being arranged.

If purchased flowers can not be placed in water for several hours, the best way to keep them fresh is to place them in a strong plastic bag with some water in the bottom. Secure the bag with a rubber band. Another method is to wrap flowers in damp newspaper. If travelling by car, place the flowers in the coolest spot.

"A life with love will have some thorns, but a life without love will have no roses."

CUT FLOWERS

The ends of woods stemmed flowers such as roses or chrysanthemums should be crushed with a heavy object or the stems slit up 1"(2.5cm) before arranging.

Before putting the flowers in water, snip off the end of each stem. When flowers are first cut, the sap in the stalk congeals and seals the cut end preventing it from absorbing water.

When buying cut flowers such as chrysanthemums or daisy types, always look at their centre. Green is freshly cut and yellow means they have been cut for some time.

If roses are wilting, cut 1cm off stem, wrap in paper, plunge stems into boiling water for approximately 10 seconds, then put into a vase filled with cold water.

Roses can often be perked up by floating the whole stem, head and all, in warm water for half an hour.

Extend the life of carnations by keeping them in a cool place. Add a dash of soda water and a pinch of sugar to the water.

Spiky flowers like lupins or gladioli should have the top three or four buds removed to prevent the head of the spike bending over and let the remaining buds open properly.

Foliage and ferns should be submerged in a bath of cold water for several hours before arranging.

To revive dropping tulips or roses, wrap tightly in newspaper and put up to their necks in water as hot as the hand can bear and leave until the water cools.

To prevent tulips from drooping too quickly after purchase, put pin pricks in the stem just below the flower head.

To prevent tulips drooping, add a pinch of starch to the water. Or place a copper coin in the bottom of the vase.

To revive drooping flowers add an aspirin to every pint of water used in the vase.

Singe the stems of poppies over a naked candle flame to make them last longer.

"In joy or sadness, flowers are our constant friends."
Kozuko Okakura

Never arrange daffodils and irises in the same vase.

Cut the stems of daffodils above the white part as only the green part of the stem can take up water and place in very cold water in a cool place for an hour.

Daffodils and narcissus have a thick sap oozing from the end of the stems when they are cut. Wipe it off before placing the stems in water. Keep these flowers separate from other flowers when they are being conditioned as the sap can affect other flowers.

Stand the stems in 3"(7.5 cm) water for at least six hours before arranging.

Bulb flowers prefer shallow water. If daffodils or narcissus are placed in deep water, the thick stems can become water logged, the stems shrivel up and the petals go papery.

"I think the sweet pea is a frivolous flower
and leads a butterfly's life,
it wanders anywhere, and clings to anything,
and has not any definite aim or ideal."

Helen Milman

CUT FLOWERS

Don't place flowers in direct sunlight, over radiators or on top of television sets. Keep in a well ventilated part of the room.

Prolong the life of fresh flowers in a warm room by adding a few ice cubes to the water twice a day.

When changing the water in a vase of fresh flowers cut off 1/4(5mm) from the stems before returning to the vase of fresh water.

A flower preservative helps destroy bacteria in the water. If a preservative is not used, the water needs to be changed and the stems cut on an angle daily. If a preservative is used, the stems do not require cutting and water needs changing only about twice a week.

Flowers like freesias and spray carnations have lots of buds. By using a preservative in the water, it helps develop the buds to open.

Add a small piece of charcoal to the water in a vase to keep it odourless. A few drops of bleach added to the water prevents the water becoming stagnant and it does not harm the flowers.

Don't place flowers near fruit as fruit gives off a gas which prematurely ages flowers.

Remove dead flowers as these give off gases that affect the others.

Non-scented flowers last longer.

Remove lily stamens as soon as the bloom is sufficiently open as the pollen can damage fabric and polished wood surfaces.

If the flower head is too heavy and the stem is hollow, put a thin garden cane or straw inside the stem to support the bloom.

"Flowers leave some of their fragrance in the hand that bestows them."

Chinese proverb

FLOWER BOXES

These are available in a variety of materials including wood, plastic, metal, terracotta. Wooden flower boxes provide better insulation than plastic or metal, with Cedar being the best as it is the most resistant to rot. Pine is much less expensive but this should be treated. Avoid using commercial wood preservatives, especially creosote

For window boxes, construct a wooden container to fit the window sill, line it with a plastic sheet and make a few drainage holes inside. Fill it with pots of plants rather than planting directing into the box. This will make it easier to change planting arrangements if required

Make sure the pots put into the box and the box itself have drainage holes, or the plants will become waterlogged.

If plants are to be placed directly into the window box, the box should be at least 8"(20cm) deep to allow for root growth and to prevent the soil drying out too quickly.

Line boxes well with newspaper to help stop the soil drying out.

In summer the box will need watering every day, aim to keep the soil moist but never waterlogged.

Choose low growing plants if you want maximum light from your window. Climbers are another option as they can be trained against the wall around the window.

If the box is sited in an exposed position on a wall or balcony, fix it with brackets or strong wire as strong winds can damage unsecured boxes leaving them in a dangerous position.

Prick over the soil surface of tubs or containers holding long term plants. This will break up the hard crust and allow easier penetration of water air and nutrients.

Sprinkle gravel over the soil in windows boxes and hanging baskets. This will prevent windows being splashed with mud during heavy showers.

"Flowers in a city are like lipstick on a woman- it just makes you look better to have a little colour."

Lady Bird Johnson

Hanging Baskets

Hanging baskets allow for increased gardening in a limited area. By suspending the plant in the air and allowing it to cascade over the sides of the pot the plant takes on a different quality than if it were growing on the ground.

When using a wire basket, or other container with open sides it is best to line it with damp sphagnum moss before filling it with soil. This not only gives the basket a neat appearance but it also prevents the soil from falling through the large openings. A well drained soil should be used, such as a mixture of 2 parts peat, one part sand and one part vermiculite.

Line hanging baskets with fir trees leaves. Cover with black polythene before filling with compost. The fir keeps its colour and smells pleasant when watered.

Placing a hanging basket directly in front of a window will cause lopsided growth, so it needs turned occasionally.

Watering is also important. If you have hanging baskets outside or on a screened patio you will need to water it frequently because of air movement.

A wide variety of plants can be used - trailing plants or plants that produce runners can be mixed with other plants.

Put used teabags in the bottom of hanging baskets before adding compost. They are an excellent fertiliser and retain water. Line flower pots with damp paper when planting to help preserve moisture

Hanging baskets need watering twice a day; to make this easier, consider attaching them to a pulley system, available from most garden centres.

Water hanging baskets by putting ice cubes on the top, moisture is slowly released as the ice cubes melt. Ensure these do not touch the plants as this may cause damage.

If soil in hanging baskets becomes too dry, add a squirt of washing up liquid to the water. This helps the water to enter the compost instead of just running off.

"Life is a flower of which love is the honey"

DRIED FLOWERS

Any dried plant material can add to an arrangement so don't overlook twigs with interesting shapes, sedges, grasses, or weeds.

Baby's breath, Thistles, Yarrow, Goldenrod, and a few other flowers will dry naturally if hung upside down in a dry, warm area.

The flowers should be picked before they are in full bloom since they will open slightly while drying. Foliage should be removed from the stem.

Hang flowers upside down in groups of 8 to 12 stems, out of the sun, in an area that is warm, dry, and has good air circulation. Flowers are ready to be used when they are crisp.

Many flowers can be preserved with the use of desiccants.

Silica gel is the most widely used desiccant because it is easy to work with and dries the flowers quickly.

A widely use desiccant is a mixture of two parts borax to 1 part silver sand or silica gel

In borax mixtures, flowers take longer to dry than in silica gel and it may be difficult to dry delicate flowers with high water content such as rose buds.

Flowers may be dried with desiccants when they are in bud or just prior to full bloom when they are at their peak of colour.

Artist pastels may be used to add colour. Finely grate the pastels into a dust. Mix dust from various colours to achieve a colour similar to the natural flower colour. Place the dust in a plastic bag and insert the flower, holding on to the stem. Dust the flower with the pastel and remove it from the bag. Shake off all excess dust.

The flower stem should be cut to 1"(2.5cm) and a wire stem inserted before the flower is dried.

"Flowers grow in inches, but are destroyed by feet"

DRIED FLOWERS

Use an airtight container to dry flowers. Cover the bottom with 1"(2.5cm) of desiccant and place the flower, with the wire stem looped below the flower, into the desiccant.

Care should be taken when covering the flower with desiccant so that the petals retain their natural position.

Gently sift the mixture over the flower using a skewer or fine paintbrush to ensure that the grains go into every crevice.

Continue this process, shaking the box occasionally, until the flower is covered with 1/2"(1.2cm) of desiccant.

Cover the container tightly with an airtight lid and leave in a dry place until the flower has completely dried.

The length of time required will depend on the desiccant and the type of flower. Carefully pour off the desiccant and gently shake off all excess. Use a soft brush to remove the finest particles.

Another method to preserve flowers and other plant materials is using a microwave oven. Microwave drying, takes only a few minutes and the dried material looks fresher and more colourful than obtained by other methods.

Flowers should be placed in a supportive substance before placing in the microwave oven so that natural form is retained. Silica gel, borax mixtures and expanded clay cat litter all work well. Silica gel however is the preferred substance.

Use only glass, paper, or special microwave containers in which to hold the flowers and desiccants. Do not cover the container.

Always place a small cup of water in the oven before cooking to prevent excessive drying.

Cooking times vary, depending on the characteristics of the leaf or flower. After cooking, flowers must be left in the drying agent for several hours, and for some specimens an overnight standing period is recommended.

*"Will is the root, knowledge is the stem and leaves
and feeling is the flower."*

Sterling

When using a microwave oven, it will be necessary to experiment with length of cooking time and length of time that the dried flowers should remain in the desiccant before removal.

Spray dried flowers with hair lacquer to prevent them dropping.

To fluff up dried roses, hold rose head over a steaming kettle and gently tease out petals.

Foliage such as beech should be preserved in a solution of 1 part glycerine to 2 parts very hot water. Split the stems up 2"(5cm) and stand them in 2"-3"(5-7cm) of this solution.

Leave them until the leaves become shiny, adding more of the solution if necessary. The time will vary from a few days to several weeks depending on the type and condition of the foliage.

An easy method to dry seed pods, berries, grasses and hydrangea flower heads. Remove all the foliage. Stand them in a vase with a little water in it. Do not replace the water. They will dry out but still retain their colour.

"January storms of wind and rain
Bring the bitter ice and snow
Yet even while the frosts remain
Under the trees the snowdrops grow"

GARDEN HINTS

Dirty vases shorten the life of cut flowers considerably. Soak vases overnight in bleach to remove bacteria.

If you want to use Oasis again store it in water. If it is allowed to dry out it will not absorb the water properly the next time it is used.

Clean block-type paving by emptying a shovel full of sharp sand on to the paving area. Vigorously brush over the surface, sweep and then hose away any excess.

To remove moss and slime from patios, brush with a solution of one cup of washing soda crystals to every pint of hot water. Be careful not to splash on plants.

Use kitty litter or sand to melt ice on your walkways instead of salt. When the ice melts, the salts runs off and can burn the roots of neighbouring plants and shrubs causing problems when they begin growing in spring.

An old hot water bottle filled sparingly with foam rubber chips is a handy kneeling pad for long gardening jobs.

Save wooden ice cream spatulas, lollypop sticks or plastic knives to use as garden labels. Write on them with a ballpoint pen or waterproof marker.

Make labels from coloured plastic bottles and colour code different types of plants. Or cut labels from ice cream cartons or margarine tubs and write on them with a waterproof marker.

Plastic plant labels that have been written on using permanent ink can be reused if they are soaked in a 75% bleach solution for a couple of weeks. Wash thoroughly before using again. Alternatively, use a pencil to mark labels, these can then be used again by erasing the name.

To "age" new garden statues, smear with natural yoghurt. Algae will quickly cover the item making it look older.

If you are using wicker baskets outside, give them three coats of yacht varnish to protect them.

"Cares melt when you kneel in your garden."

HOUSEPLANT CARE
&
MAINTENANCE

*What a desolate place would be
a world without a flower!
It would be a face without a smile,
a feast without a welcome.
Are not flowers the stars of the earth,
and are not our stars the flowers of the heaven."*
A.J. Balfour

HOUSEPLANTS

With houses being centrally heated, better insulated and having large picture windows or conservatories, more interesting and colourful plants can be grown indoors.

Houseplants fall mainly into two categories, foliage plants and flowering plants.

Foliage plants can be green-leaf, coloured or variegated. Green leaf plants are hardy and generally easy to grow. Rubber plants would be the exception.

Coloured foliage plants need constant higher temperatures and more humid conditions which may be difficult to maintain in houses.

Variegated leaf plants grow well indoors though they need to be placed in an area with good light.

Flowering plants will flower year after year if cared for properly and that includes re-potting.

Flowering pot plants are garden or greenhouse plants specially grown to flower indoors mainly during spring and winter. They are purchased when the buds have formed and have a slight showing of colour. They can flower for several weeks and do not need any special care other than warmth, watering and deadheading.

Once they have finished flowering they should either be discarded, planted out in a greenhouse border or if hardy planted in the flower garden.

Most indoor plants come from tropical or arid regions. Plant selection is important to determine whether a particular plant will only survive or thrive in a chosen indoor location.

The eventual height and shape of a plant should also be considered when choosing plants.

It is important to begin with good quality, healthy, pest-free plants. Check that leaves possess good colour for the species, with no brown tips or margins. Watch for insects, mites and signs of disease.

"It's perfectly okay to be a late bloomer"

Daily exposure to light of 8 -16 hours is needed for plants to thrive. A southern exposure indoors provides the greatest light intensity, then western, eastern, and northern. Direct sun is not recommended but nets or venetian blinds can be used as a filter.

Do not leave plants between window glass and curtains during winter nights.

Plants with variegated foliage require more light than plants with green foliage. If light is insufficient, variegation may be lost. Flowering plants also require higher light intensity.

Symptoms of insufficient light intensity or duration include: weak growth; long, spindly stems; poor colour in older leaves; and leaf loss or failure to flower.

Instead of leaving your houseplants in the same place turn them around regularly. It will enable all parts to get their fair share of light and grow into a round and bushy shape.

Avoid placing plants near heat sources

Central heating is generally run on a time switch, rooms can have a fluctuating temperature and low temperatures, this can slow the growth of some delicate plants.

Avoid draughts and provide fresh air. Symptoms of cold damage to plants include leaf spots or blotches; downward curled foliage; slowed growth; and root rot.

Excessively high temperatures cause yellowish green foliage with brown, dry edges or tips and spindly growth. Insect, mite and disease problems may develop quickly under warm conditions as well.

Humidity or moisture in the air is necessary and beneficial to most tropical houseplants. To increase the indoor humidity, lightly spray the plant's foliage with water.

Another method of increasing humidity is to place the pots on a wet bed of gravel. Double potting may help, sink pots in a larger container, then fill in between pots with moistened sphagnum moss.

"Gardening: another day at the plant."

WATERING HOUSEPLANTS

Use warm water with a drop or two of mild detergent added to clean a plant's foliage. Rinse washed leaves with clear water to remove soap film. Plants with hairy foliage should be dusted rather than washed.

Polish houseplant leaves with cotton wool soaked in milk

More house plants are killed from improper watering than from any other single cause. When plants are over-watered, the soil remains saturated and root systems are unable to function properly because of lack of oxygen in the soil.

Soil-borne bacteria and fungi invade the roots and eventually destroy the entire root system. The plant may struggle for months before it succumbs.

Plants that do not receive enough water become stunted and woody, the leaves turn yellow and finally fall.

Watering frequency depends on the kind and size of pot, soil mix, environmental conditions and plant species, size and stage of growth.

Soil mixes high in organic materials such as peat retain more water and plants grown in these mixes will not have to be watered as frequently as plants grown in mixes containing high amounts of sand or vermiculite.

High temperature and low humidity will increase the rate of water loss from a plant.

Generally, plants should be watered when the soil becomes dry to the touch . However, some plants, such as ferns, need to be watered before the soil becomes dry to the touch. Cacti and succulents can tolerate greater dryness; let the soil become crumbly dry for several days before watering.

To determine when a plant needs water, feel the soil mix with your finger-tip. If the soil mix is slightly moist wait another day or two and retest before watering.

Another method to determine when to water is to use the weight of the container. A dry container and soil mix will be lightweight compared to one that has just been watered.

"Don't throw away the old bucket until you know whether the new one holds water."

Swedish proverb

The two methods of watering are - applying water to the top of the soil or watering from the bottom of the container with the use of a saucer or tray.

Watering constantly from below brings nutrient salts to the soil surface. An excess of these salts may accumulate in the upper soil layer in four to six weeks and this can result in burning of the upper roots and/or stem.

Once a month water thoroughly by applying enough lukewarm (room temperature) water until it runs out of the bottom of the pot. This leeches out excess fertiliser salts in the soil. It also exchanges the air in the soil mix.

Do not allow drainage water to seep back into the soil mix; empty the container of excess water as soon as the pot drains completely.

If a plant's soil mix is excessively dry and hard to rewet, try double watering. Water once and then again half an hour later; or place the pot in bucket filled with water. Remove it from the bucket when the soil surface is moist. Allow the pot to drain after using either of these methods.

Do not water plants with softened water as this may add sodium and chloride to the soil mix and cause plant damage

Most plants thrive well in soil mix that is moderately moist. After watering thoroughly, allow the soil mix to dry to a slightly moist condition before watering again.

The most likely cause of older plant leaves dropping is under-watering whereas the most likely cause of younger plant leaves going yellow is over-watering.

Put broken eggshells into a watering can, fill with water and leave overnight. This will extract the nutrients making an excellent and cheap plant feed.

Save the water from an aquarium each time it is changed and use to water houseplants.

Use a plastic funnel to water houseplants and the water goes straight into the soil and not over the leaves.

"God made rainy days, so gardeners could get the housework done."

WATERING HOUSEPLANTS

Always water plants in the evening during hot weather so that the water can soak in around the roots and not evaporate.

Occasionally water Azalea plants with a mixture of two tablespoons white vinegar to 1ltr(2pts) water. Azaleas like acidic soil.

To keep plants watered whilst you are away for a few days, place one end of a pipe cleaner into the soil by the plant and the other end into some water. The pipe cleaner will gradually draw up the water.

During a longer stay away, place a towel in the bottom of the bath and add 1" of water. Place house plants on top of the towel and they will draw up the water as required

"He who is born with a silver spoon in his mouth
is generally considered a fortunate person
but his good fortune is small compared
to that of the happy mortal who enters this world
with a passion for flowers in his soul."

Celia Thaxter

Pots must have drainage holes in the bottom whether they are clay, plastic, or ceramic.

New clay pots are porous and allow air movement through the sides of the pot. This allows the soil to dry and provides oxygen to the root system.

Plastic and glazed ceramic pots are nonporous and do not allow air movement through the sides; the soil holds moisture longer and therefore does not need to be watered as often as soil in clay pots.

Soil can be kept from falling through the drainage holes by placing a piece of newspaper or broken pottery over the hole.

Do not put a layer of gravel or pieces of broken clay pots in the bottom of pots with drainage holes as this slows down water movement through a pot rather than aiding it. A small piece of broken clay pot can be placed over the drainage hole to prevent soil from draining through the hole.

Containers without drainage holes should have a layer of coarse gravel placed in the bottom to allow a space for excess water.

To "double-pot", pot the plant in a container that has a drainage hole. Put several inches of gravel in the base of a larger decorative pot and place the potted plant on it.

Used pots can be reused if cleaned thoroughly or heat sterilised. Scrub with a 10% solution of chlorine bleach and water, using a stiff brush or wash pots in the dishwasher.

Corks from wine bottles are easily sliced up with an old pair of secateurs or used whole to keep the drainage holes clear without adding too much weight to hanging or standing pots. Use them in winter to cover the topsoil of pot plants against frost damage

"Successful gardening is doing what has to be done
when it has to be done
the way it ought to be done
whether you want to do it or not."

Jerry Baker

SOIL & FERTILISER

Houseplants must have a loose, well-drained soil. Packed soils should be loosened from time to time, being sure not to damage the root system. Re-pot plants in spring when growing conditions are best.

Most plants thrive in a mix containing: one to two parts potting soil, one to two parts moistened sphagnum peat moss and one part coarse sand or vermiculite.

Soil from the garden can be used in a mix if it is first "pasteurised." The soil should be moistened 24 hours prior to heating. Place soil on a baking sheet, 2"(5cm) deep, and heat in an oven at 180°F for 30 minutes. If soil is high in clay content it does not make the best mix.

If after watering a plant most of the water drains out of the pot then the plant's soil ball is shrinking. This happens when the potting mix is allowed to dry out and pulls away from the sides of the pot. To avoid this, change to a potting mix with less peat moss in it and water more regularly.

To correct an existing problem, immerse the entire pot in water to make sure the root ball gets plenty of moisture. If the shrinkage is severe, re-pot the entire plant.

Fertiliser should only be used on healthy, well-watered and actively growing plants. Use complete water-soluble fertilisers.

Dilute fertiliser to about one tenth the recommended label rate and use this solution to water plants at every watering. Once a month, flush pots with clear water to wash out excess salts.

Houseplant fertiliser stakes are a continuous feed method as some fertiliser dissolves with each watering over a period of three to twelve months. However, use these with caution since it is not easy to correct a salts problem should it occur. If the plant goes into a dormant phase or if dark and cloudy weather occurs, these fertilisers can't be leached quickly from the soil mix.

Most houseplants do not require fertiliser during the winter since there is little rapid growth at this time. Feeding once or twice during the winter months will be adequate for most plants.

"The best fertiliser is a gardener's shadow"

White discoloration near the top or bottom of pots or a crust of salts at the soil line may indicate that the plant is being over fertilised and/or over-watered. If salts are high and the soil excessively dry, root damage or death is possible

Pinching stimulates new growth from buds lower on the stem. It is commonly using on vining and bushy plants.

The growing stem tip is removed, just above a node. Pinch with your thumb and forefinger, or use a sharp scissors to make the cut.

Mature plants can be pinched to produce dense, bushy growth, especially on fast growing, soft-stemmed plants with long, lanky stems. Once side shoots form, they can be pinched to promote even more new growth.

Re-potting should be done only as needed, during spring or summer when the plant is actively growing. Do not re-pot ailing or dormant plants or those with flower buds or open flowers.

A plant needs re-potting if roots are growing out of the drainage hole or "surfacing" in the pot, if the plant wilts shortly after watering, or if it requires frequent watering. As roots grow they compact the soil, decreasing the pore space which holds water and air for the root system.

Choose a pot 1"-2"(2.5-5cm) larger in diameter. With each 1"(2.5cm) diameter increase in pot size, the volume of soil nearly doubles.

If a plant is re-potted into too large a pot, the root system is surrounded by a large volume of soil which can become excessively moist and slow to dry out, leading to root rot.

The plant to be re-potted should be slightly moist. Remove it from its pot and gently disturb the root system with your fingers so that roots are headed outward from the root ball. Place some soil mix in the new pot and position the plant so it will be at the same depth; fill in around the sides of the ball with new soil mix. Water well so excess water drains out of the container.

For plants in large containers that are impossible to re-pot, carefully remove the top two or three inches of soil and replace with fresh soil every two years. This process is known as top dressing.

"Old gardeners never die, they just go to pot"

CARING FOR HOUSEPLANTS

It is beneficial for some plants to be put outdoors during the summer months but it is important not to move plants outside until the danger of frost is over.

If the weather is very sunny then put the plants in a shady area so that they are gradually exposed to the sunlight.

Plants outside will grow rapidly, and require frequent fertilisation and watering if rainfall is not adequate.

Plants should be carefully inspected for insect or mite pests before bringing them indoors. Control any pests found as indoor conditions may help to increase them rapidly.

Winter is a good time to check houseplants, potted patio plants stored in the garage and greenhouses for tiny, soft-bodied pests. Get rid of pests by hand or vacuum them off.

Remove and destroy plant parts or the entire plant if it is totally infested. Discard infested soil and clean pot or container as well.

When using chemical pesticides, note that few pesticides are registered for indoor use on houseplants. Read labels carefully for where and how to use a pesticide. If indoor use is not listed on the label, take the plant to be treated outside away from children and pet traffic areas. Leave the plant outside a day or two after spraying.

Isolate infested plants from others so pests don't spread from plant to plant.

Place aluminium foil around the base of a plant to disorient winged pests like aphids and prevents them from landing.

Paint a small dish yellow and fill it with water to attract and drown winged aphids.

Avoid insect infestation of your houseplants, add a little garlic powder when watering them. Remove greenfly from plants by spraying with soapy water or infused with garlic. Always test the spray on a small area first in case it damages the plant.

"You will catch more flies with a spoonful of honey than with a gallon of vinegar."

HOUSE PLANTS FROM FRUIT

Many unusual plants can be grown from the seeds of fruit such as peaches, dates and avocado.

Put peach and date stones in small pots of compost, cover with black polythene and leave to germinate at $18^{\circ}C/64^{\circ}F$. Peach stones must be kept at $4^{\circ}C/39^{\circ}F$ for a few weeks before planting.

For avocados to germinate insert two or three cocktail sticks or matchsticks into the sides of the stone. Suspend the stone over a jar of water with the pointed end upwards. The base of the stone should be just touching the water. It will take 6-8 weeks for roots to appear.

Plant the stone with the roots down 2"-3"(5-7cm) deep in compost, in a large pot. Keep in a warm, humid place with plenty of light. After a few weeks a single shoot will emerge and develop long slender leaves. Avocado plants will grow rapidly, pinch out the growing shoot when the required height is reached. Re-pot annually.

Pips of citrus fruit such as lemons, oranges and grapefruit can produce plants. Plant the pips as soon as they are removed from the fruit.

Fill a 4"(10cm) pot with compost and water well. Leave to drain. Plant 4-6 pips 1/2"(1cm) deep. Cover the pot loosely with a polythene bag secured with a rubber band. Keep at $18^{\circ}C/64^{\circ}F$ for a few weeks until shoots appear. Remove the bag and keep at the same temperature until the plants are well established. Plant out singly into 4" pots. These plants will grow to 3'-4'(1m) bushy plants with a lovely smell.

To grow the top of a pineapple into a plant, cut the top of the fruit below the first row of pips on the skin.

Fill a 4"(10cm) pot up to 3/4"(1.9cm) below the rim with compost. Sprinkle a thin layer of coarse sand on top. Place the pineapple crown on the sand and sprinkle a little more compost over the fleshy part.

Cover the pot with a polythene bag and leave in a shaded place at $18^{\circ}C/64^{\circ}F$ for 8 weeks. The leaves should look fresh or new leaves will appear. When the plant looks well established remove the polythene bag and re-pot into a larger pot. The plant can grow to 2'(60cm).

GARDEN HINTS

To make brand new containers look immediately old, coat them in natural yoghurt and leave in the sun.

Cut top and bottom off large plastic bottles to use as sleeve and arm protectors when pruning or hedging.

Give old pottery vases a new look by sanding them lightly and coating with any colour of matt paint.

Use an old coffee jar to spread dry fertiliser. Drill holes into the plastic lid, fill with fertiliser shake where required.

A natural way of removing flying insects/eggs etc. in greenhouses is by using a vacuum cleaner.

A piece of wood placed upright in a plastic water barrel will prevent the barrel splitting when it freezes.

To reduce the amount of compost in a large plant pot, place a layer of broken crockery, then broken polystyrene to fill large plant pots to one-third of the depth of the pot.

Reuse chopsticks to stir right to the bottom of watering cans, support young tomato plants and as a dibber for pricking out.

Don't discard your worn out wellingtons. Cut off the legs and wear them on your arms when pruning prickly shrubs.

Useful string can be made from old VCR tapes. Remove the spool with the tape on it, from the cassette case. Carefully stretch a short length of tape at the time until it becomes string. Leave any tape not required on the spool. Use this "string" to tie young plants and trees to their support stakes.

To give young vine plants a place to grow upward on, a trellis can be placed about 3ft(1m) above the plants and the "string" can be hung from the bottom of the trellis. This gives the vines a way of climbing to the trellis for support.

When fixing a trellis to a wall use batons to raise it from the surface. This allows the air to flow freely around the climbing plant and reduce the problems of mildew and other diseases.

*I*TS *P*LANTING *T*IME

Plant five rows of P's
presence, promptness, preparation,
perseverance, and purity.

Plant three rows of Squash
squash gossip, squash criticism,
and squash indifference.

Then sow five rows of Lettuce
let us be unselfish and loyal, let us have good fellowship
let us be faithful to our club,
let us all work for new members,
and let us be kind to one another.

No garden is complete without Turnips:
turn up for all meetings, turn up with a smile,
turn up with new ideas,
and turn up with the determination to make everything count for
something good and worthwhile.

GARDEN HINTS

Punch holes in the bottom of old plastic or paper cups and use to plant seeds.

Make a small propagator from an old plastic sweet jar, lay it horizontally and place a plant tray inside, replace the lid.

Cut the base of clear plastic soft-drink bottles to make a mini cloche to protect planted out seedlings from slugs and cold. Unscrew the tops gradually to acclimatise plants to cooler air.

Cut cardboard milk cartons in half horizontally to plant sweet corn, beans, sweet peas etc. When planting out, cut the sides away with scissors to avoid damaging the roots.

Plastic cartons that takeaway food comes in make excellent seed trays for standing pots on in cold frames.

Cardboard egg boxes are excellent for planting individual seeds - one per hole. When planting out the seedlings, cut the box into it's compartments and plant each in the ground, the cardboard is biodegradable and will disintegrate.

When sowing fine seeds, mix with sand for easier sowing.

Leave cans of water to warm up in a greenhouse to water tender seedlings.

Soak seeds in a cup of cool tea, then place into the refrigerator for 3 days. They will now be ready to plant.

When growing sweet peas from seed, fill a pot two-thirds full with compost and water well, top up with dry compost. Plant seeds 1/2"(1cm) beneath the surface of the compost. This way the seed with draw up as much water as required and will not rot.

To enhance the germination of morning glory or lupin seeds, nick each seed with a pair of nail clippers. Place the seeds on a lightly dampened paper towel, fold the towel over and place inside a plastic zipper bag for a day or so before planting.

"All the flowers of all the tomorrows are in the seeds of today and yesterday."

Chinese proverb

Seeds and Transplanting

When using pots or trays that have been used previously, disinfect them by scrubbing them in warm soapy water, rinse well.

When planting seeds indoors it is important to use a sterile medium. Garden soil can be used but it should be sterilised and as this is a tedious procedure it is probably better to use a commercially available mix.

Firm the mixture down to 1/2"(1.2cm) from the top of the container using a flat piece of wood or the base of another pot.

Sow the seeds thinly and evenly. Cover large seeds with 1/4"(6mm) sieved compost, while smaller seeds just need a light dusting of compost. An old coarse flour sieve is ideal for sieving the compost.

Water the compost by standing the tray or pot in water half way up its sides. Remove from the water when the compost is well wet.

Label the containers and cover with glass, polythene or a clear heavy plastic bag. Individual pots can be placed inside plastic bags closed with a rubber band. This keeps the planting medium both warm and moist.

Put trays and pots in a warm shady place.

If moisture forms inside the bag or on the glass wipe it off.

Seeds can take from five days to three weeks to germinate. Most seedlings show a pair of small round or oval leaves.

When seedlings sprout remove the covering otherwise, you risk suffocating the young seedlings. Place the tray or pot into a position where there is more light but out of direct sunshine.

Seedlings need a lot of light. If they receive insufficient light they become tall and spindly or "leggy."

"Many things grow in the garden that were never sown there."

Thomas Fuller

SEEDS AND TRANSPLANTING

Place near a large window that receives full sun. In dull weather artificial light should be used as well. Use bulbs recommended for growing plants and place them 12"(30cm) above the seedlings. If using only artificial lighting, the lights will need to be kept on at least 14 hours a day. Fluorescent tubes don't produce as much heat reducing the chance of seedlings drying out quickly.

The medium should be kept moist, but not wet or soggy. Water from the base, allowing the medium to soak up the water like a sponge.

To prevent seedlings from drying out it is important to water carefully. If using total artificial lighting it is quite easy to predict how often watering is required. When using a sunny windowsill, it will help if the containers are placed on a raised bed of gravel spread across the bottom of a large pan with a small amount of water. Make sure the water level is below that of the gravel so that the plant containers rest on the gravel and not on the water.

It is important not to start seeds indoors too early. If they outgrow trays or small pots try thinning them and transplanting the largest to bigger pots, but it is easier to plant them outside just as they become large enough to survive transplanting. This is generally four to six weeks after sowing, when they have at least two sets of true leaves. If aiming to plant in the first week of May start the seeds around mid-March. Toward the end of this period, you may want to provide your seedlings a little food in the form of a weak, water-soluble fertiliser.

As soon as the first true leaf appears from between the seed leaves the seedlings are ready to be transplanted.

When transplanting, fill a seed tray with compost. And mark out planting holes with a dibber or pencil to ensure even spacing.

The holes should be spaced over 1"(2.5cm) apart in each direction. A standard seed tray will accommodate 40-90 seedlings.

Using a plant label or a narrow piece of plastic lever up a small clump of seedlings. Catch a seedling by one leaf and use the dibber or pencil to tease it away from the clump.

Drop the seeding into the prepared hole and firm the compost around it gently with the dibber.

When the tray is full of seedlings, label and water with a fine-rose attachment on a watering can.

Place the tray in a cold frame or on an indoor widow ledge but away from direct sunshine for a few days. Then move into direct sunlight for a few weeks until the plants are well established and healthy.

Before planting out, the seedlings must be hardened off. Move to an unshaded cold frame or leave them under a covered porch or patio for a few days. Or cover them during night-time with newspaper or a light sheet.

When transferring transplanted seedlings either from a garden nursery or seeds started indoors, make sure the weather conditions are favourable before placing outdoors.

Prepare the proper environment before planting out seedlings. Good soil preparation is the single most important thing you can do for your flowers. Loosen soil to at least 6"(15cm), add organic matter (such as peat moss, compost, or manure) and mix well. Rake to level.

Plant when the soil is moist, if the weather is dry then water the soil the day before transplanting.

Knock the seed tray on the ground to loosen the compost and leave a space to insert a trowel or fingers beneath the compost.

Break away a row of plants and gently separate each plant ensuring there is a good root system.

Dig a planting hole with a trowel, make it wide and deep enough to accommodate the plants root system.

Set the plant that the base of the stem is level with the surface of the soil. Fill the hole and firm down the soil around the plant.

Encourage bushy plants by pinching out the growing tip.

"In every failure lies the seeds of success."

Deepak Chopra

SEEDS AND TRANSPLANTING

The spacing between plants depends on the species of plant. A general rule is to space plants apart, half their eventual height except for plants that spread, these should be spaced full height apart.

Don't smother new plants with too thick a soil blanket.

Nourish young plants well during growth spurts. Water with diluted water-soluble fertilisers or manure tea from a watering can, or side dress the plants with compost.

Weeds rob seedlings of nutrients so constant weeding is important to ensure sturdy plants.

Once plants flower, keep the colour coming by removing, faded flower heads (deadheading).

If a flowering plant blooms and then fades, revitalise it by shearing off the faded blooms and one-third of the top growth. Fertilise and this restores the performance and blooming of "past their prime" plants.

It helps to pinch out the centre of young flowering plants, such as petunias and fuchsias, to encourage more bushy side growth. Tall delphiniums, sunflowers, and dahlias may need to be tied to stakes.

When moving perennials it is a good time to acquire more plants. Pull off the side shoots and transplant in a new location where the soil has been loosened and well watered. It is advisable to do this on a cloudy day.

When choosing plants from a garden centre, always pick healthy stock. Select stocky, deep green plants with buds slightly showing. Spindly plants in full bloom make poor transplants. Avoid plants with discoloured or wilted leaves.

When transplanting, select plants that are about as tall as they are wide, dark green in colour, vigorously growing, and free of spots or lesions on the leaves, indicating disease problems.

If bedding plant transplants have become root bound (roots are crowded and encircling each other), gently loosen the root ball at planting time.

"Scatter seeds of - Happiness, Hope, Kindness and Love."

Set the root ball of the transplant into the hole, filling in around it with soil. Leave enough space between seedlings to allow each plant to reach its mature potential without crowding its neighbours.

Transplant larger nursery stock the same way you would seedlings. Control invasive plants, such as tansy, mint, or bamboo, by planting them in their pots -- cut the bottom out of the pot first -- to contain their runners.

Do not fertilise transplants for several weeks, Instead, water thoroughly, using a splash of B vitamins to help overcome transplant shock. Water regularly until plants show new growth, indicating they're rooting and surviving well.

Grow varieties of plants that require little or no staking and plant closely so they support each other.

Before planting shrubs in the garden, lay the plants out in their pots roughly in the place where you plan to plant them. This way you'll be able to check if they are in the right places before any heavy work has been done.

When bringing delicate plants indoors to protect them from cold weather, put several into the same pot to take up less space.

If tender buds or shoots become frozen, thaw them out slowly by spraying with cold water before the sun shines, otherwise they may get scorched.

Planting seeds too closely together or over-watering can cause damping-off disease where the base of the seedling turns brown and dies.

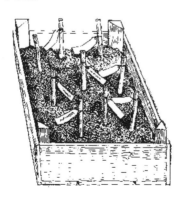

"And so it criticised each flower,
This supercilious seed;
Until it woke one summer hour,
And found itself a weed."

Mildred Howells

BULBS

When buying bulbs always select carefully. Good bulbs are plump, firm and free from blemishes. They should also be a good size (for the type) as if they are too small they may not flower in the first year.

Bulbs are should be planted in clusters. They look good under a tree, in a tub or in window boxes.

If planting bulbs in grass remember to choose low growing varieties. To achieve a random look, scatter the bulbs onto the lawn and plant where they fall. Remember bulbs planted in lawns make mowing more difficult.

Bulbs not planted deep enough do not thrive well. As a general rule they should be planted at three times the depth of the bulb. If the bulb measure 2"(5cm) from top to bottom, they should be planted 6"(15cm) deep.

When the flowers are finished the dead flower heads should be cut off before they turn to seed to prevent the plant being weakened for the next year. Leave the stems to turn brown and die off naturally, this will allow nourishment to be returned to the bulb for next year's flowers. Don't trim the leaves off or tie them down.

If you need to remove the bulbs to make way for other planting, carefully lift out the bulbs and replant them in a corner of your garden with wire netting beneath them. Lift and replant in autumn.

Daffodil bulbs should be in before the end of October. Small varieties developed from wild daffodils should be planted in holes 3"(7cm) deep, other varieties at 6"(15cm) deep.

Tulips can be planted from October until the end of November in holes about 4"(10cm) deep.

Don't plant tulips in the same spot two consecutive years. Never plant tulips and lilies together as they suffer from the same diseases.

"When you're green your growing.
When you're ripe, you rot."

Ray Kroc

After tulips flower, pull away leaves as soon as they are yellow and withered, to prevent disease entering the bulbs. Apply a liquid fertiliser to build the bulbs up ready for next season. Feed once a week for a month.

Snowdrops can be planted as bulbs before the end of September in holes 3"-4"(7-10cm) deep, If possible, plant them immediately after flowering whilst still in leaf.

To give bulbs a boost, apply a light feed of a general fertiliser, once they have flowered and the leaves have started to die down.

Crocuses should be planted before the end of September at about 2"-3"(5-7cm) deep.

When planting bulbs indoors for Christmas flowering, buy 'prepared' bulbs as these have been treated to speed up their development. The middle of September is generally considered to be the best time for planting to ensure flowers for Christmas

Put some well soaked bulb fibre or potting compost into a pot leaving enough space to allow the bulbs to be placed inside with the tips just below the rim of the container. They should be placed close together but not touching.

Cover with bulb fibre or compost and water well. The container should then be placed in a cool spot - in a shed or bury it in a shady corner of the garden. Darkness is not necessary but coolness is. Do not put in a black plastic sack as this encourages mould.

After 10-12 weeks young green shoots should appear (these will be paler if the pot has been kept in the dark). When the shoots have reached about 2"(5cm) in height, bring the pot into a cool room and they should flower in time for Christmas.

Plant bulbs in the garden, in a buried flower-pot. This can then be easily lifted when bulbs have finished flowering.

When storing bulbs over the winter make sure to separate them into different colours and label the boxes to make it easier for planting arrangement in the spring.

"Gardens are the result of a collaboration between art and nature."

Penelope Hobhouse

LEGENDS & LORE

Clover was one of the first plants cultivated by man and has been highly regarded since ancient times. The three-leaf shamrock is associated with the Christian Trinity and is the national emblem of Ireland. The rare four-leaf clover is also a Christian symbol with its four leaves representing the cross. It is supposed to ward off evil including witches. Each leaf represents different aspects of happiness; one leaf for fame, the second wealth, the third a faithful lover and the fourth for excellent health. Wearing a four-leaf clover in your shoe will bring you a mate. Four-leafed clovers are well known for their luck and magical charm but according to old wives' tale they are not found; they make themselves known only to lucky people.

According to Christian legend the daisy sprung from Mary's tears during the flight into Egypt. It has always been associated with purity, innocence and loyal love. According to German folk-lore daisies picked between 12 noon and 1p.m. have magical qualities. They should be dried and carried as a good luck charm.

The name of the dandelion comes from the French term for a lion's tooth (dent-de-lion). To carry your thoughts to your sweetheart, blow the feathered seeds off the puffball. To dream of a dandelion is supposed to be bad luck.

Ivy is a lucky plant. If it grows on a house, it protects those within from witchcraft and evil. In Christmas decorations it is as lucky to the woman, as holly is to the man, and therefore should never be omitted if all the family are to share alike in the blessings of the season. The wood of the plant was supposed to have the power of separating water from wine when these were mixed together. The leaves, roots and wood of ivy were used in a number of folk-remedies, some practical and some mainly magical.

In Greek burials it was the custom to cover a dead body with violets as a symbol of both the beauty and the transitory of life. In literature violets are often associated with modesty and simplicity.

"Advice on dandelions: If you can't beat them, eat them"

The Outdoor Garden

When a man sits down in front of a garden,
or strolls around in it,
he steeps himself in delight.
Because the garden is a paradise
where a garden owner and a landscape gardener
share the same dream in their common culture.
Man first made a garden to try to
produce a paradise in this world.
The garden seems to be a paradise of the other world
somewhere out of sight.

Masaaki Noda

Garden Soil

A soil test is the most efficient and money-saving step toward better gardening. A soil test measures levels of nutrients (nitrogen, phosphorus, and potassium) that are available for plants, as well as what your soil lacks.

The test also indicates your soil's pH level -- the relative acidity or alkalinity -- that affects how plants take up nutrients and thrive. Soil pH ranges from 1.0 (acid) to 14.0 (highly alkaline), with 7 being neutral. In certain areas, soil is typically more acid (in rainy areas) or more alkaline (in dry areas) and needs to be amended accordingly for plants to thrive there. To raise too-low pH (acidic): add lime, dolomite limestone, or wood ashes. To lower too-high pH (alkaline): add horticultural sulphur, composted oak leaves, or pine needles.

Check the pH of garden soil before planting expensive or unusual shrubs and perennials. Many plants thrive in any soil but there are some that dislike acidic soil. Use a simple pH testing kit to determine what plants are suitable in your garden.

Never add lime to soil without first checking its pH to ascertain if it is required.

Never apply manure and lime to soil at the same time. They will react together and produce harmful ammonia. Allow at least two months between applications of lime and manure.

To determine the texture of soil, rub some soil between moistened fingers - a sandy soil feels rough, a clay soil feels greasy and a loam somewhere in between.

When digging soil in the autumn, don't break down the clods as the winter rain will make them compacted. Leave the clods rough and they will disintegrate slowly.

Improve clay soil by double digging and incorporating plenty or organic matter as you work it.

Use manure within a year as a large proportion of the nutrient will be leeched out.

*"To forget how to dig the earth and to tend the soil
is to forget ourselves."*

FLOWERS AND SHRUBS

Keep deadheading flowers and they will keep blooming for much longer, instead of producing seeds early in the season.

To trap aphids put some water and oil in a yellow dish and set it in the garden - they love the colour yellow and when they land on the water the oil will prevent them escaping

Plant garlic or parsley under rose plants to keep aphids away.

Pinch off the tendrils of Sweet Peas to improve their flowering capacity.

Bury fuchsia's in the winter to protect them from the frost.

Use toilet roll centres to plant sweet peas, runner beans or garden peas as they need a good root run.

To deepen the colour of your blue hydrangea, simply grow the plant with iron nails around its base. This alters the pH balance of the soil which then changes the colour of the flower itself.

Do not dead head hydrangea as they give protection for next year's buds. Prune when the danger of frost is past.

When re-potting or moving prickly plants or conifers, cut the bottom off an old compost bag to form a tube which you can then place over the plant. Tie the top and bottom with string, this will condense any awkward branches and also protect your arms.

A circle of twigs 20"(50cm) high, provides a better support for border plants than a single stake, and is less obtrusive.

Do not clear away old vegetation or foliage around plants in borders as this gives protection in severe weather.

"A tree is known by its fruit; a man by his deeds.
A good deed is never lost;
he who sows courtesy reaps friendship,
and he who plants kindness gathers love."

Basil

FLOWERS AND SHRUBS

When planting up summer annuals in pots or baskets, plant up half a dozen extra pots in ordinary flower pots and nurture them in the same way. As the summer progresses and bare areas appear where plants have either died or perennials haven't survived the winter, simply position the pots in the gaps and fill the borders instantly again.

To help when re-potting plants into larger pots, place the current pot into the larger pot and push compost firmly into the gap between the two. Gently remove the inner pot to leave the correct size hole into which the plant can be dropped.

To prevent slugs getting to plants in containers, smear outside of container with petroleum jelly or WD40.

When planting container grown plants, disturb the roots as little as possible so that they continue to benefit from the compost they are grown in. Water as usual after planting.

When planting new climbers and ramblers for the spring, plant them about a foot from the supporting wall and lead them to the wall via a cane. This will give the roots room to develop properly and help to give years of healthy growth

Use old tights or stockings - cut into strips - to tie up plants, rather than twine which can slice into stems.

Do not remove dead leaves from plants damaged by frost as they are nature's way of protecting new young shoots.

Never move or plant anything if the ground is frozen. Wait until the soil warms up.

To kill grass or weeds growing around low carpeting plants, make up a mixture of grass weed-killer as directed on the container. Add a squirt of washing-up liquid. Put on a pair of strong rubber gloves and then a knitted mitten or thick sock. Dip your hand into the mixture and let the sock or mitten soak. Squeeze out the excess and then touch the weeds or grass. The slimy solution will stick to the weeds and not destroy the plants.

"A weed is a plant that has mastered every survival skill except for learning how to grow in rows."

Doug Larson

OUTDOOR PLANT CONTAINERS

Choosing a container for plants is important. Plastic pots are cheap, light and durable and they keep the soil moist, however, they can turn brittle and crack.

Terracotta pots are made from baked clay and are very attractive, however they are heavy, break easily and are subject to frost damage.

Glass fibre containers have a wide variety of moulds and colours. They can look like stone but are much lighter. They are strong, durable and repairable but are expensive.

Reconstituted Stone are crushed stone moulded into shape. Imitation classical urns and vases are very attractive but extremely heavy and should be used with caution in roof gardens or balconies.

If using new concrete plant containers, leave them outdoors for a few weeks to weather fully as some concrete can contain setting agents that may be harmful to plants.

Wooden half barrels are useful plant containers. Line the barrels with strong plastic to stop the compost coming in contact with the wood. Make drainage holes both in the plastic and the barrel.

When using heavy plant containers make sure to position them in their intended final sites before filling as they are difficult to move. If they do have to be moved put lengths of old scaffolding pipes under the pot to use as rollers.

Take the wheels off old whellie suitcases, shopping trolleys or old pushchairs and fix them to the bottom of heavy patio pots. This will mean that they can be easily moved around the garden or pathways.

To reduce the weight of compost in a large pot, fill the container with empty plastic bottles to a depth of 8"(12cm). Cover with a layer of polythene making holes in it for drainage. Fill to the top with compost.

When stacking terracotta pots place a few sheets of newspaper between them to prevent the pots from jamming together and making them difficult to separate.

"Tomorrow is the busiest day of the year"

LAWNS

The most important ingredient in a good lawn is the preparation of the ground before sowing or laying turves.

Good drainage is essential though the soil itself must be moisture retentive.

For the grass to become established the lawn must be properly fertilised, watered regularly in dry weather and weeds eliminated.

A lawn can be sown or laid at any time of the year when the weather isn't frosty or dry. The best months are April and September.

When choosing turf for the lawn, make sure that it is free from coarse grass and weeds as these are difficult to eradicate.

The thickness of the turves is no guide to its quality. Generally thin turves properly laid, root more rapidly than thick ones. All turves purchased should be of equal thickness.

Lawn turves are delivered in rolls. Since these are heavy to move they should be dropped as close as possible to where they are required.

Lay the turves as soon as possible after delivery as the grass tends to yellow after five days, depending on the weather.

Use an old tenon saw to cut the turf to size and shape. This is a much safer way to cut the turf rather than using a knife that could slip and injure the person using it.

When laying the turf avoid placing a short piece at the end of a row where it will fray. Move a large piece to the end and put the smaller piece next to it.

Stand on a wooden plank when working with lawn turves to avoid damaging them.

When the area has been completely turfed, roll it twice, the second time at right angles to the first. Do not roll again until the turf has rooted and then only lightly.

"Cultivate what you want to grow."

To prevent cracks or shrinkage water newly laid turf once or twice a week with a garden sprinkler.

If cracks appear in a lawn after laying or during the summer months they can be filled with a fifty-fifty mixture of sand and non-soil compost or peat. Re-seed at the same time. Repeat procedure when necessary.

In the springtime replace any patches of turf that have failed to root or seed these areas when the weather is right.

When seeding a lawn choose a calm day. The surface of the soil should be dry but moist underneath.

To ensure even coverage, sow half the seed across the area and the remainder up and down.

After sowing a lawn lightly rake in the seed to avoid exposure on the surface and it will germinate better. Do not roll.

Do not walk on the lawn when the grass is frozen. The grass blades will break and leave brown marks until the spring.

Repair bad patches of lawn with surplus pieces of turf acquired when making new flower beds etc., cut to size and fit into the gap. Add plenty of compost into the cracks, and water well.

To kill toadstools or fungi on the lawn, water with diluted Jeyes Fluid, it doesn't damage the grass.

The lawn should be fed in the springtime to encourage the grass growth. A good time to use lawn feed is when it is raining lightly. The rain prevents the feed from scorching the grass.

Regular mowing is important. When the growth is most vigorous in late spring the lawn should be mown frequently. This encourages thicker grass cover which will help to reduce weed and moss growth.

Do not mow grass when it is very wet. Avoid cutting very close. Grass should be left slightly longer in dry weather and in spring and autumn.

"Should I weed the lawn, or say it's a garden"

Garden Hints

Apply a teaspoonful of salt directly onto a weed such as dandelion in your lawn to kill it.

Avoid splashing creosote on plants when treating woodwork as it can cause severe leaf scorching.

The secret of getting a new ivy to cling to your walls is to cut it hard back after planting. New shoots get a grip straight away - old ones never do.

Hang nets under trees in the autumn to catch some of the falling leaves and save having to rake them off the ground.

When raking leaves in the garden, sweep them into a pile and water lightly with a watering can. Soggy leaves will not fly away in the wind and more will fit into the wheelbarrow or sack.

When gathering rubbish in the garden or house roll a piece of cardboard into a tube and place it in a dustbin liner. The cardboard must be able to expand when released in the liner so that it can stand on the ground unaided. This will enable you to have both hands free when loading the bag with rubbish. As you fill the bag raise the cardboard slightly until the bag is full. Remove the cardboard, which can be used again, and tie the liner as usual.

When carrying heavy loads such as compost in the wheelbarrow always load more at the front of the barrow (over the wheel). That way the barrow will move better and not make your arms painful.

Use an empty, cut-off lemonade bottle to water your growing bags. Turn the bottle upside down in the growing bag and pour the water directly into the funnel that the bottle makes. The water will run directly into the growing bag and not leak out on to the floor.

"Garden: One of a vast number of free outdoor restaurants operated by charity-minded amateurs in an effort to provide healthful, balanced meals for insects, birds and animals."

Henry Beard and Roy McKie

PONDS

When building a new pond, remember that siting it in full sun will encourage the growth of algae, so position it in a lightly shaded area.

When the hole has been dug for a pond, use whole newspapers soaked in water to line it instead of using sand. The papers can be moulded around any contour. Or use old carpet. Both will protect the liner for many years.

Do not line a pond with normal polythene sheeting as it will tear easily. Use purpose made butyl rubber sheeting which should carry a guarantee against leaking.

Install an overflow pipe in a new pool as heavy rainfall could cause the water to spill over the edge.

Take a pair of old tights, cut the legs off and place one leg inside the other. Fill the tights with aquatic compost and tie off the open end. To plant - burn a hole in the tights with a match at various points, and plant your aquatic or marginal plants through the holes. Locate the bag around the edge of the pond to suit requirements. The plants will soon grow through the tights and the tights will soon be hidden.

A ball left in a pond before an overnight freeze will help to stop the pond from completely freezing over. If the ball is removed in the morning it leaves an air hole for fish and a water hole for other animals.

Remove algae or blanket weed from a fish or garden pond by rotating a rough barked stick in it. To make the algae easier removed from the stick cut a lengthways groove it in and the algae can be cut off with scissors. Use the algae as compost in the herb garden.

After placing plants in a garden pool wait three weeks for the water and plants to settle before introducing fish..

To keep that green slime from collecting in the birdbath or fountain, add a few copper pieces or coins.

If pot plants are close to a pool they should be moved away when applying liquid fertiliser as it could harm fish in the pond and it also encourages algae growth.

"The frog does not drink up the pond in which he lives."

LEGENDS & LORE

Some of the oldest beliefs concerning plants and flowers are bound up with moon magic. Plants and seeds should not be put into the ground when the moon is waxing, as the moon grows, so do the seeds.

In Somerset, a county well known for its cider, there is a method of predicting the apple harvest: apple blossom in April signifies a good crop but if the trees don't bloom till May the yield will be poor. At harvest time when cider was taken into the fields for the harvesters the first drop must be poured into the ground for good luck.

Hazel was a holy tree in the days of Celtic paganism, associated with poetry and knowledge, fire and fertility. Its nuts are still connected in country belief with love and child-birth, and are used in divination on Halloween night. Rods made from its wood were formerly employed to detect hidden veins of metal in the earth, and water-diviners today often use forked hazel twigs for their work.

The source of the name birch has not been clearly established. Birch rods have been used since ancient times to punish children and others. Birch wood has been used for furniture, wooden spoons, tool handles and broomsticks. American Indians used the water-resistant birch bark for canoes and wigwams. In northern Europe the birch was a sacred tree.

The fig tree is a sacred tree and figs an important fruit to many ancient people. It is still sacred in India, China and Japan and Moslems call the fig "Tree of Heaven" and revere it. The Greeks and Romans believed that the fig was a gift from the god of wine and agriculture.

The elder has been used by man, since before recorded history. The pith can be easily removed from elder sticks leaving a hollow pipe suitable for making music. In medieval Europe the elder was associated with evil and witches. It was considered dangerous to sleep in the shade of an elder or plant one near a house. The berries make a lovely wine though most parts of the elder are poisonous when eaten raw.

"Though a tree grows so high,
the falling leaves return to the root"

HEDGES & TREES

In the door yard fronting an old farm-house
near the white-washed palings,
stands the lilac-bush tall, growing
with heart-shaped leaves of rich green,
with many a pointed blossom rising delicate,
with the perfume strong I love,
with every leaf a miracle
and from this bush in the door yard,
with delicate-coloured blossoms
and heart-shaped leaves of rich green,
a sprig with its flower I break.

Walt Whitman

HEDGES

A garden will benefit from having at least one length of hedge. It will give privacy and shelter from strong winds.

In a small garden hedges should be kept to the minimum. A fence covered with ivy, honeysuckle or some other climbing plants may be preferable.

Remember that tall evergreen hedges can block the sun and air to other plants in the garden.

Hedging plants should be chosen on the basis that they will grow quickly, survive close planting, hardy and suitable for the soil in the area.

Hedges can be grown from one species of plant or from several. All plants grown in a mixed hedge must be of similar habit.

Flowering shrubs planted close together and minimally pruned can form a hedge but will take up more space than a regular hedge.

When planting a hedge dig the strip of ground 3'(1m) wide and two spits deep. Add a dressing of yard manure or compost to the bottom.

Plant deciduous hedging in October or November, providing the weather is mild damp and calm. Do not plant in frosty or cold drying weather. Planting can be done up until March.

Evergreen hedging should be planted between mid September and mid October but if this is not possible then April or early May.

All plants should be well furnished with shoots from the base. Bare leggy plants are difficult to make bushy.

Any long tap-roots should be shortened and the tops of evergreens can be cut back.

"Someone's sitting in the shade today because someone planted a tree a long time ago."

Warren Buffett

Generally plants should be 18"(50cm) high and planted 18"(50cm) apart in the row. Some varieties may need less or more spacing so check with the garden centre when buying the plants.

If a dense hedge is required two rows 18"(50cm) apart can be planted alternating the plants so that they are not opposite each other.

Plants should be put in a little deeper than the soil line on the plant and the soil well firmed in around them.

Spring planted hedging may need to be watered. Put a mulch around them when the soil has warmed up to help conserve moisture. Spray lightly in the evenings of hot days.

In the early stages of growth shoots arising from the base should be stopped when they are 9"-10"(22-25cm) long. This ensures that a series of lateral shoots are sent out up the whole height of the hedge and encourages a thick base.

Most hedges should be trimmed twice a year, in early summer and in late summer or early autumn. This leaves it neat and tidy over the winter for growth to start again in the spring.

Keep the hedge at a height that is easy to reach without having to use steps or trestles. A hedge between 5-6ft(1.5-2m) is ideal.

To keep a base of a hedge leafy cut into a pyramid shape in spring, so that the top is narrower than the base. If a hedge is pruned wider at the top than the bottom the lower part will be shaded and the foliage will fall off allowing the top growth to spread, compounding the problem. The narrow top also makes it easier to trim.

When using a ladder to cut a high hedge it will be necessary to prevent it from sinking into the foliage. Get a piece of timber approximate 4ft(1.3m) in length and nail two short lengths of drainpipe the same width as your ladder, at right angles (making a "H" shape). Place the top edge of your ladder into the drainpipes. The plank spreads the weight across the hedge.

"A hedge between keeps friendship green."

French Proverb

HEDGES

There is a growth retardant that can be purchased and sprayed on the hedge after cutting to slow down the growth for the rest of the season.

If a hedge is too dense, cut it back to the main stems on one side only. Let the hedge recover and produce new growth for a year, then cut back the other side.

If a hedge is too tall, cut back every second shrub to within a few inches of the ground. New shoots should sprout around the severed trunks. Cut back the remaining shrubs the following year.

Tree wounds over 1"(2.5cm) in diameter can be dressed with a tree wound dressing available from most garden centres.

To stop this protective dressing from cracking with sun exposure it is important to make sure the wound is dry before applying the dressing to ensure good bonding.

Check the coating several times during the first year and retreat if cracked.

As well as clipping, hedges should be kept free of pests, diseases and weeds.

Leave a space of 1'-2'(30-60cm) between hedges and the foliage of other plants.

"It used to be thought that our love of plants was an impractical but pure passion . But now, in the age of environmental crisis, we're discovering that gardening is essential to human life."

Jacqueline Heriteau

HOW TO PLANT A TREE

A tree's dormant period from late autumn after leaf drop to early spring before bud break is the best times for planting.

Prepare for planting by calling the local utility companies to locate your underground lines. Whatever form of tree you plant, the instructions are similar. The following method refers to balled-and-burlapped and container-grown trees.

Measure the diameter of the tree's root ball with the shovel handle. Remove sod that's twice as wide as the root ball. Set the tree aside (pick it up by the root ball, not by the trunk).

Dig a planting hole. Make sure it is deep enough so that the top of the root ball will align with ground level. Loosen soil in the bottom of the hole and around the sides. Peel the burlap back from the trunk but leave it on the root ball; it will decompose eventually. Remove any containers, plastic, twine, or wire encasements. Centre tree in the hole.

Refill the hole with soil. Do not fertilise. Crumble dirt clods, then settle the soil and eliminate air pockets around roots by watering the hole as you fill it. After the hole is completely back-filled and watered, apply mulch. Water again in a week, then again every week (unless 1"(2.5cm) of rain falls) through the first growing season and prior to winter.

When planting bare rooted trees and shrubs, spread the roots out like an umbrella, twisted roots stunt growth. As you cover the roots with soil shake the plant from time to time to allow the soil to drop down well between them. Water well after planting.

Put support stakes in before you plant a new tree to avoid the possibility of damaging the roots.

To prevent snow damaging small conifers, when it is forecast tie the branches to the trunk with string or old nylon tights, however, do not leave them tied for more than a day or two.

When planting trees or other large plants make sure they don't adversely affect your neighbour's house or view.

"The apple doesn't fall far from the tree"

FRUIT TREES

Crab apple are the most commonly used ornamental fruit tree. Cherry and plum trees make beautiful additions to the landscape, they flower in early spring and then produce a crop of tasty fruit in the summer.

The best age to buy fruit trees such as apples, peaches, cherries, plums and pears for planting in the home garden is 1-2 years old.

Fruit trees can be planted at any time when they are dormant, usually from November to the end of February,

Do not plant fruit trees or shrubs near the vegetable garden. Their needs are different especially the specific spraying for disease control.

Dessert apples, gooseberries and strawberries should be grouped together as they require only a limited amount of nitrogen. Cooking apples, plums, bush and cane fruit need more while blackcurrants will require a large amount.

Raspberries and gooseberries like moderate shade while other fruits like full sunshine.

Mulching fruit trees helps to conserve moisture, control weeds, adds plant food as the mulch decays, and catches the fruit when it drops, preventing bruising.

Young developing trees often set fruit that take the nourishment needed to build up the tree framework. Most of these fruits should be removed at an early stage.

Sometimes older fruit trees set more fruit than they can hope to develop. Some thinning should be done but not until the natural shedding has been completed generally around mid July.

Branches of old fruit trees should be well propped to prevent them breaking when laden with fruit.

Fruit trees are quite hardy but the flowers are easily damaged by frost. To avoid this, cover the trees with a light piece of material or newspapers.

"A seed hidden in the heart of an apple is an orchard invisible."

If blossoms are only slightly frozen, cover to protect them from the early morning sun as it is quick thawing that causes most damage.

To evaluate pollination in apples, slice an apple crossways, there are five seed pockets with the potential of two seeds in each. If there are 8-10 fully developed seeds then you should have a good crop. If there are less then better pollination is required from more bees in the garden or a different variety of fruit tree.

Soft fruit should be picked when it is cool and dry. Early in the morning after the dew has lifted but before the sun warms the fruit. Plums should also be picked dry.

If apples or pears are to be stored then they are best picked dry otherwise they should be spread out to dry after picking.

Check the ripeness of apples by gently lifting the fruit with the palm of the hand, while still attached to the tree. When ripe the stalk will detach itself easily.

If the garden is more than 600'(175m) above sea level it will be difficult to grow fruit trees satisfactorily, unless they have plenty of protection.

To help keep fruit trees free from pest allow chickens to feed under the trees to eat the insects and larvae.

Store apples and pears separately as apples should be left undisturbed while pears need to be checked regularly.

Fig trees need their roots confined. Plant in a 3ft(1m) cubic hole, line the sides with concrete slabs and fill with rubble.

"I think that if you shake the tree, you ought to be around when the fruit falls to pick it up."

Mary Cassatt

LEGENDS & LORE

In ancient Greece and Rome the hawthorn was linked with hope, marriage and babies. At wedding ceremonies the bridal attendants wore its blossoms and the bride carried a bough.. However in medieval Europe the hawthorn was regarded as an unlucky plant and that bringing it into a house would cause the death of a member of the household. Anyone uprooting or cutting down a hawthorn bush in a "fairy fort" would have bad luck.

The laurel is associated with fame and achievement. It is also believed that a person standing under a laurel tree would be shielded from infection by the plague, from lightening and witches.

The oak tree has a widespread association with thunder gods, this is probably due to the fact that oak seems to attract more lightening than other trees. To Northern European people the oak leaf cluster was a token of heroism and victory. In literature the oak denotes strength, masculinity, stability and longevity.

The olive tree not alone provides oil but also, food, fuel for lamps, as medicine, an emollient for dry skin and anointing oil for religious purposes. The olive is regarded as a symbol of peace, wealth and as a sign of safe travel.

The weeping willow is a well-known symbol of unlucky love and mourning in the Western world. In the Orient it has been associated with the springtime regeneration of nature, eternal friendship, patience, perseverance and meekness. It is dangerous for cattle to eat willow leaves.

The traditions with mistletoe are many. Kissing under the mistletoe is first found associated with the Greek festival of Saturnalia and later with primitive marriage rites. Mistletoe was believed to have the power of bestowing fertility. In Scandinavia, mistletoe was considered a plant of peace, under which enemies could declare a truce or warring spouses kiss and make-up. In some parts of England, the Christmas mistletoe is burned on the 12th night lest all the boys and girls who have kissed under it never marry. And for those who wish to observe the correct etiquette: a man should pluck a berry when he kisses a woman under the mistletoe, and when the last berry is gone, there should be no more kissing!

THE VEGETABLE PATCH

*In green old gardens, hidden away
From sight of revel and sound of strife,
Here I have leisure to breathe and move,
And to do my work in a nobler way;
To sing my songs, and to say my say;
To dream my dreams, and to love my love;
To hold my faith, and to live my life,
Making the most of its shadowy day.*

Violet Fane

RAISED BEDS

Raised bed gardening has many benefits. It can save space, reduce water loss, and discourage weeds. Reducing foot traffic in the growing area reduces soil compaction. And concentrating organic matter in a defined area builds soil productivity.

Creating raised beds takes considerable amount of work at the beginning so try one or two beds first. And then if you are happy with the results, add more next season.

To make simple raised beds, choose a well-drained site with adequate sunlight and a nearby water source. Beds should be only as wide as can be easily worked from either side, usually about 3'(1m) and as long as required.

If the soil is compacted, do not start to prepare the bed until the soil is dry enough to work.

Spread a 2"-3"(5-7cm) layer of organic material over the soil surface. Organic material can include compost, sawdust, ground bark, leaves, chipped pruning materials or manure. Adding an additional source of nitrogen helps the organic material break down more efficiently. Rotavate or dig in the organic material, nitrogen supplement and soil down to a depth of at least 6"(15cm)

With a shovel and rake, shape the bed. Shovel a walkway area, about a 18"(45cm) wide, to a depth of 6"(15cm). Add the excavated soil to the top of the bed. Finished raised beds should be at least 8"-12"(12-30cm) higher than the paths. Level the top of the bed with a rake.

Put sawdust, bark or old carpet on the paths between beds for a less muddy walking surface.

Raised beds don't have to be contained by wooden boards. Beds could be raised to waist-high level, if stooping is a problem. Remember that the higher the raised bed is, the quicker it will dry out, so monitor moisture carefully.

Once the beds have been properly built, light digging or forking will then create a suitable bed for planting. As time goes on, soil will keep loosening and you will be able to garden almost year round.

"A garden is a work of art in progress."

VEGETABLES

Instead of the hard work of getting up turf, and then having the problem of disposing of it, lay old paving slabs over the area to be made into a bed. Leave it for a month or more, then take the slabs up. All the grass will have died off. Dig the new patch and dig in some compost. It works best in the winter months when the ground is wet.

Dig the vegetable garden during a dry spell in late autumn or early winter. The frost will make the soil crumbly and workable, ready to plant the seeds in the spring. Firm down the surface with your feet and level it off with a rake.

Potatoes are the best crop to sow in a new vegetable garden. They help to clear the ground of weeds because during their cultivation they need plenty of hoeing and weed clearing. They also produce dense cover to inhibit weeds. Their extensive root system breaks up the soil. If the garden was previously grassland the potatoes may suffer from wire-worm damage.

Make a careful decision on how many vegetables of each type to plant. A lot of water is lost through leaves so in a dry year large brassica can draw out valuable soil moisture.

If the garden is small choose cut-and-come-again plants such as leaf lettuce and spinach which will continue to crop from the same plant.

A three course rotation plan should always be developed . Different groups of vegetables make different demands on the plant food in the soil as well as requiring different cultivation.

The allotted garden should be divided into three and each plot cropped in turn - pod bulb and stem crops (peas, beans, leeks, celery), green crops (cabbage, broccoli, Brussels sprouts, kale) and root crops (carrots, turnips, potatoes, beetroot).

Runner beans and onions are the only exceptions and can be grown in the same plot two or three years in succession

*"Gardening adds years to your life
and life to your years."*

VEGETABLES

Seeds should be covered with soil 2 - 4 times their own smallest diameter. For early sowings, and in clay soils, cover a little less than the normal depth.

When sowing carrot seeds, distribute a layer of ground coffee grinds. This not only helps the carrots to grow straight but also helps to prevent carrot fly

Seedlings should be transplanted as soon as they form their first true leaves (these are the third and fourth leaves to form) and before they become crowded in the tray or pot.

Rows of small vegetables should be thinned as soon as the individual plants begin to crowd each other and before there is the slightest chance of their becoming "leggy" for lack of light and air.

To prevent peas being eaten by pests, fill a short length of plastic guttering with compost and sow peas along the length as normal. Hang guttering out of reach of pests. When seedlings are 2"(5cm) tall, slide the compost and seedlings into a shallow trench in the garden

Runner bean and snap peas shoots should be supported with canes once the plants are around 6"(15cm) tall. This will encourage them to climb.

If cloches are not used to protect young pea or bean seedlings then lightweight mesh netting must be placed over the row to protect from birds.

Dig the roots of beans and peas into the ground in the autumn as they are high in nitrogen and beneficial to the next rotation crop.

Always use two hands to pick peas to avoid pulling the plant out of the ground.

Pinch out the tops of broad bean plants to encourage growth, plenty of flowers, this also discourages black fly.

Avoid planting carrots in very stony ground, in fresh manure or in heavy clods as these cause misshapen roots.

"Gardening is a matter of your enthusiasm holding up until your back gets used to it."

Sow carrot seed sparingly to minimise the need for thinning. Any disturbance of foliage attracts the carrot fly.

After thinning carrot plants or hoeing around them, remove all traces of thinnings and water lightly with a watering can or hose to dampen down the aroma from the foliage.

Carrots, beets, and turnips should be stored in a cool, dark place, packed in sand or slightly moist peat moss, or in boxes covered with bags containing sand, leaves, or peat moss.

When planting cucumber, pumpkins or marrow, place a plastic collar around the seed (use an old bottomless pot or the centre of a large plastic mineral bottle). When watering the plant do not water inside the "collar" and this will keep the area dry around the plant and avoid "collar rot".

Another method is to submerge a pot next to each plant, when they need watering, pour water directly down below soil level.

Do not plant string beans, corn, cucumbers, squash, pumpkins or spinach seeds until the soil is well warmed.

Avoid watering cucumbers with cold or chlorinated water, keep a container of water in your greenhouse.

*"Hoeing: A manual method of severing roots from stems
of newly planted flowers and vegetables."*

Henry Beard

VEGETABLES

Plant cauliflower seeds in individual pots and transplant carefully without disturbing the roots. Space the plants 4"(10cm) apart and 8"(20cm) between rows. Never allow the plants to dry out.

Brassica plants benefit from being planted deep in order to establish a strong root system to support their large heads. Plant with the soil up to the level of their basal leaves.

To inter crop vegetables, plant rows of quick-growing crops, such as lettuce, radishes, or spinach, between widely spaced, slower growing items, such as celery, peas, and tomatoes. If carefully planned inter cropping can result in producing more food from a given area. This can also be done with trees and shrubs, berry bushes and herbs can be planted between fruit trees.

In a small garden it is best to plant early potatoes. Each year use fresh certified seed tubers as saved potato tubers can have virus contamination.

For better results, choose seed tubers about the size of a hen egg rather than cutting up large ones. Early potato tubers should have two sprouts (rub out any excess). Main crop tubers should have numerous sprouts.

Make sure that potatoes are always well earthed up as this stops them getting frosted or being exposed to the sun and becoming green and poisonous.

Harvest spinach frequently as it is prone to bolting especially in light soils and dry conditions.

To improve the growth of leeks add a little soot to the soil

When planting leek plants, trim the root and leaf tips. Drop the plant into a 6"(15cm) deep hole and fill the hole with water.

Weeding between onion rows should be done by hand as hoeing will damage the shallow roots.

Small onion sets will produce onions that are less likely to bolt.

"He who plants a garden, plants happiness. "

Chinese Proverb

Plant onion sets, shallots or garlic with a trowel, do not push the bulbs into the soil. With shallots and garlic leave the shoot showing through on the surface.

Plant garlic cloves in January, poke 4"(10cm) holes in the ground with the end of a rake and drop the garlic cloves into them.

Squashes, pumpkins, and onions require dry storage. The squashes and pumpkins should be "cured" for a week or two, and then stored on a shelf in a cool, dark room Onions should be kept in the dark, in a dry place when they have been dried for several weeks after harvesting.

Save some seeds from small red peppers and plant two or three seeds at a time in yoghurt pots. When they are a couple of inches high re-pot in a medium sized plant pot. You will soon have an attractive indoor plant - and a supply of chillies.

Pick Brussels sprouts from the bottom of the stem as the more mature sprouts are below the younger ones. Cut off the sprouts rather than pulling them to avoid damaging the stems.

Watercress can be grown in an area of fairly damp soil. Over-watering will diminish the flavour.

When feeding tomatoes with liquid feed this can scorch the leaves. To avoid this happening pour from the watering can using a piece of 11/4"(3cm) drain pipe as a funnel directing the feed straight to the base of the plant, away from the leaves.

Pinching out the side-shoots on tomato plants is a good way to propagate them. If the side-shoots are pulled off the plant when they are about 4"(10cm) long, and planted in moist soil, they will usually root and produce extra plants for free.

Outdoor tomato plants should be of the bush variety as they are less labour intensive and do not require tying in or side-shooting.

Shake 1 teaspoon Epson Salt around tomato plants or peppers to green up the foliage.

Let my words, like vegetables, be tender and sweet,
for tomorrow I may have to eat them"

VEGETABLES

When thinning larger plants, use a knife to cut the stem at ground level. This thins the plant population effectively and does not damage root systems of the remaining vegetables as pulling out unnecessary plants will do.

Don't waste vegetable thinnings - small onions may be used as scallions or spring onions. Baby carrots can be added whole to soups and stir-fries. Salad greens, mustards, cabbage and broccoli thinnings can be used in a mixed salad. Or the thinnings of many kinds of vegetables can be used for transplanting, if additional plants are wanted

A thin coat of newly mown grass cuttings spread around their bases will help control caterpillars on brassica (cabbage, broccoli etc).

Cabbage may be stored in a cool dark place between 35o-40o. Hang by the roots from hooks in the roof. They can also be stored in an outdoor mound or barrel - cabbages are piled in a mound with the roots up, on a bed of sand, and sand is packed around and over the heads.

When hoeing the ground, only disturb the top 1/2"(1.25cm) of soil. Going deeper than this will cause more weed seeds to germinate.

"In order to live off a garden, you practically have to live in it."

Frank McKinney

THE HERB GARDEN

I plant rosemary all over the garden
so pleasant is it to know
that at every few steps one may draw
the kindly branches through one's hand,
and have the enjoyment
of their incomparable incense,
and I grow it against walls
so that the sun may draw out
its inexhaustible sweetness
to greet me as I pass

Gertrude Jekyll

LEGENDS & LORE

Chicory was believed to have the power of making its possessor invisible. It could also open doors or boxes if it was held against the locks. These charms, however, would only work if the plant was gathered at noon or at midnight on St James's Day (July 25th). It had to be cut with gold and in silence; if the gatherer spoke during the operation, he would die, either at once or shortly afterwards.

Parsley should never be transplanted, but grown from seed. It takes seven weeks to germinate and one belief is that it grows down to the devil and then up again. When the parsley does grow, it should be picked, not cut; and never give it away as misfortune is sure to follow. Parsley is not only a sure sign of a strong woman, but it will only grow outside the home of an honest man.

Basil stands for "animosity," and the planting method shows why. A gardener should curse with great gusto while planting basil seeds otherwise they won't grow! It is also reputed to stimulate sensuality. In New Mexico, carrying basil in your pockets is supposed to attract money to them.

Aphrodite first cultivated marjoram so ancient Greeks wore wreaths of sweet marjoram as wedding flowers. They also considered it an antidote for snakebite and if this failed they planted it on the grave to help the dead to sleep in peace.

Rosemary has been associated with memory so students studying for examinations used to wear garlands of rosemary on their heads. It is also linked with fidelity and love so it was used in wedding garlands. A rosemary plant flourishing outside a house is a sign that the wife is the boss of the household.

Sage thrives in the garden of a woman who rules her household, and her husband firmly. Another belief is that the sage plant reflects the fortune of the man of the house, flourishing when he's prospering and withering when he isn't.

"When young 'sow wild oats'; but when old, grow sage."

H.J. Byron

HERBS

Herbs can be grown in a separate part of the garden - preferably near the kitchen - or they can be grown in pots or containers or with other flowering plants. They like a sunny place and light, fertile, well-drained soil but they are generally hardy enough to be grown in most soil. Herbs are short-term plants, some are annuals and must be planted each season from seed. The perennials will need to be renewed every 2-3 years.

BASIL, also called sweet basil is a pleasant smelling annual plant with a spicy taste. The leaves are light green, tender and smooth. Basil grows well in the garden or as a potted plant. Cooks favour it for all kinds of tomato dishes. It can also be added to soups, vegetables and Italian dishes. Start basil in pots indoors or outdoors if the soil temperature is above 50oF/10oC. Cover seeds with fine soil, to a depth of only 1/8"(3mm). Gently press down the soil over seeds and water with a fine spray. Seeds should germinate in 1-2 weeks. Keep the soil moist. Shade young basil plants if the weather is sunny as they wither easily. Thin seedlings by cutting unwanted plants off at the soil surface with scissors. Basil plants should eventually be planted 12"- 18"(28-45cm) apart. After seedlings are 6"(15cm) high, pinch off the tops for bushier plants. Harvest basil leaves regularly. Water and fertilise the plants frequently. Pinch off the flowers to keep the plant from going to seed.

BAY is a large herb plant that grows into a small tree or tall evergreen bush. Its aromatic leaves are used to garnish pates, in fish dishes or in a bouquet garni to flavour soups and casseroles.

CHERVIL is a white flowered, hardy annual raised from seed. Its foliage is similar to parsley and it likes a shady area. It has a delicate slightly spicy fragrance and can be used in soups, sauces, savoury butter and potato salad.

CHIVES are small perennial, onion-like plants that grow in a clumping fashion. In early spring the leaves are topped with pink/purple flowers. Plants can be purchased or grown from seed. Established clumps can be divided and transplanted.. Garlic chives are similar in appearance to regular chives but have a slightly garlic flavour. Use chives fresh, cut off from the plant as required, use to give a mild-onion flavour.

"Plant kindness and gather love"

HERBS

DILL is an annual herb whose leaves and seeds are popular flavourings for pickles, cucumber and fish dishes. It is a tall plant with small yellow, umbrella shaped flower heads and feathery foliage, similar to fennel. Dill seeds can be planted in the autumn or early spring.

FENNEL is similar to dill but is perennial and hardier. However the plants can become very large so it is best to grow annually, It will self-seed freely. The leaves and bulb have an aniseed flavour. Use the leaves with fish and the seeds with eggs, cheese, vegetables and in cakes.

LEMON BALM is a lemon scented plant used in iced drinks and hot teas. It spreads rapidly so it should be planted in a container in the ground or frequently cut. Growing to a height of nearly 2'(60cm) its oval leaves have slightly serrated edges and clusters of small white flowers. Start from seed or small plants. It will self seed or can be propagated by root division.

MINTS such as peppermint and spearmint are hardy perennials used to make herbal tea, flavour drinks and liqueurs, and to make mint sauce. Mints are the easiest to grow perennial herbs. They grow profusely in sun or shade. Plant in moist soil in sunken pots in the garden to stop spreading. Use the leaves and flowering tops both fresh and dried.

OREGANO/MARJORAM can be grown from seed sown in the spring or propagated by cuttings. They are low growing, clump-forming slightly woody perennials. Shoot cuttings can be taken in late summer and the plant should be replaced every 2-3 years. Cut the tender tops of both herbs just as flowers begin. Add oregano to Italian-type sauces, pizza, and meats. Marjoram can be used in stuffing flavouring meats and it enhances mushroom soup.

PARSLEY is a very popular mild flavoured herb. It is a densely leafy biennial but is best grown annually from seed. There are curly and flat-leafed varieties, the curly is popular for its appearance but the flat leafed had a stronger flavour. It can be slow to germinate but watering with hot water after planting the seeds can speed up the process. Once the leaves appear it grows rapidly. Regularly used as a garnish and for flavouring a wide variety of meat and vegetable dishes.

"You have to eat a lot of parsley to be an old sage. "

ROSEMARY is an evergreen bush with leaves like long, oval pine needles. It should be trimmed frequently or renewed every few years or it will become straggly. Since it is a tender plant it should be brought indoors during the winter. The plant can be started from seed or propagated from a cutting. Purchased plants should be about 12"(28cm) tall. It is highly aromatic and used to give added flavour to lamb, poultry and roast vegetables.

SAGE is a woody perennial growing to about 2'(60cm) in height. It has grey-green, soft, furry leaves and blue flowers. Cut the plant back after the flowers are gone. It can be started from seed or propagated from cutting, layering or root division.

TARRAGON has delicate upright shoots with soft, narrow willow like leaves. It is excellent for flavouring salad dressing, chicken and fish. It is best starting with a plant but can be propagated by cuttings or root division. Should be brought indoors during the winter or else well covered outdoors.

THYME is a shrubby perennial herb. It is a small plant with very tiny grey-green leaves. Purplish flowers are formed on the ends of the stems. New plants can be started from seed (indoors), cuttings or root division. For best growth, thyme should be replanted every 3-4 years. To use, remove the top one-third portion of the plant when in full bloom and spread on newspaper to dry. Then strip the leaves and flowering tops from the stem and store in tightly closed containers. Use in stuffing's and meat dishes.

"As Rosemary is to the spirit, so Lavender is to the soul."

METHODS OF DRYING HERBS

Tender leafed herbs such as basil, lemon balm, tarragon and mint have a high moisture content and must be dried rapidly in a dark place to keep their deep green leaf shade.

Woodier herbs such as sage, rosemary and thyme can be partially dried in the sun.

DRYING HERBS
Rinse herbs in clean water and tie in bunches with string or elastic bands.

Hang upside down outside in the sunshine, in an airing cupboard, in the kitchen or in an oven at a low temperature.

BAG DRYING
To prepare plants for drying, remove blossoms from the herb plant and rinse the leaves on the stem in cold water to remove soil.

Allow plants to drain on absorbent towels until dry. Then place the herbs in a paper bag and tie the stems. Leave 1"-2"(2.5-5cm) of the stems exposed. This allows the plant oil to flow from the stems to the leaves.

Place the bag in a warm, dry location. In about one to two weeks, when the leaves become brittle, tap them free of the stems and the leaves will fall into the bag. Store leaves in an airtight container away from the light.

TRAY DRYING
Clean herbs as for bag drying but the heavy stalks can be discarded.

Put the leafed stems one layer deep on a tray in a dark, ventilated room.

Turn over the herbs occasionally for uniform drying.

The leaves are ready for storage when they are dry and the stems are tough.

"There are no gardening mistakes, only experiments."

Janet Kilburn Phillips

MICROWAVE DRYING

Use a microwave oven to dry herbs.

Place the herbs between paper towels and set them on the rack.

Close the door and turn the oven on a medium setting for about 2-3 minutes.

Then check for dryness; the leaves should feel brittle and should crumble easily. If they are not done, turn the oven on for 30 seconds longer.

Although this process actually cooks the herbs, the end product is the same as air-drying. Store the dried herbs in closed containers.

PRESERVATION

When the herbs are dry, either keep the leaves whole or crumble and pack into small jars.

Cover and label with the date, store in a cool dark place.

The shelf life of many herbs is 1-2 years but this period is shorter if herbs are exposed to light, heat and open air.

When herb seeds are to be used for cooking, the seeds should be stored whole and ground up as needed.

FREEZING

Herbs may also be frozen.

Rinse herbs in cold water and blanch in boiling, unsalted water for 50 seconds.

Cool quickly in ice water, package and freeze.

Dill, parsley, chives and basil can be frozen without blanching.

"When planning for a year, plant corn.
When planning for a decade, plant trees.
When planning for life, train and educate people."

Chinese Proverb

GARDEN HINTS

Bats are useful in a garden as they eat approximately. half their weight in insects each night. Bats are also very instrumental in plant pollination

Plant nasturtiums, dill, lavender, thyme, hyssop or sage around the base of apple trees or other plants to control aphids.

If you are having problems getting your runner beans to set, either try spraying them with sugar water or planting sweet peas in the same row. Both methods will attract pollinators.

To store and ripen green tomatoes, harvest tomatoes free of blemishes, wash and dry them. Place in a box with 4 ripe apples. Keep in a cool place around 50-60oF/10-15oC The ethylene gas produced will help ripen the fruit.

Don't throw out that old carpet, turn it upside down on a newly dug patch of soil or between vegetable beds to use it as an inexpensive weed blanket. Slit through when planting and then cover entirely with bark or gravel.

Ladybirds are a great gardener's friend. Always put them on plants suffering from aphids as they just love to eat them. To attract ladybugs to your garden plant Jerusalem Artichokes.

Although we may not like spiders, they do eat a lot of insects and without them the garden would soon be over run with pests.

Encourage the birds to come into your garden particularly with a bird bath. Birds eat a lot of garden pests and they are lovely to watch.

When filling plant pots with compost, only fill to within 1"(2-3cm) of the rim to allow room for watering.

When you've boiled eggs, use the leftover water to pour between the cracks in the path to prevent weeds growing.

Pour a line of salt where you think ants are coming in to the house, and a pile where they tend to congregate

"It takes both rain and sunshine to make a rainbow"

Working
IN THE
Garden

To garden,
you open your personal space to
admit a few, a great many, or thousands of plants
which exude charm, pleasure, beauty, oxygen,
conversation, friendship, confidence,
and other rewards
should you succeed in meeting their basic needs.
This is why people garden.
It can be easy but challenging,
and the rewards are priceless.

Tom Clothier,

FERTILISERS

An array of fertilisers can now be purchased and they are all blended for every possible type of plant and every possible circumstance.

There are three main ingredients contained in varying amounts in all fertilisers and these are nitrogen (N), phosphate (P) and potash (K).

Nitrogen encourages leafy growth. Phosphate encourages roots to form and is valuable at planting time. Potash stimulate flowering and fruiting.

Fertiliser should always be spread as uniformly as possible in the area they are required. Labels on the container should specify the dosing instructions.

Always wear gloves and wash hands after handling fertiliser.

Fertiliser for organic gardens - fill a container quarter full of barnyard manure or well-rotted compost (never use dog or cat faeces). Fill to half full with water. Over the next 24 to 48 hours stir several times during the day. After 48 hours, your fertiliser is ready to use. Dilute the liquid to a light amber colour with water. Pour 1pt(500ml) of diluted solution around each plant when setting out, or later as necessary to force growth.

When removing nettles from the garden, put them in a bucket and cover with water. Leave for two to three weeks and the resulting strongly smelling liquid makes an excellent fertiliser, especially good for tomatoes.

Place old banana skins around the base of rose plants as fertiliser.

Dissolve 1lb(450g) dried milk in a little hot water, add to 1gall(5ltr) cold water. Spray on tomatoes, lettuce and cucumber when planting and every ten days afterwards..

"Money is like manure: It's not worth anything unless you spread it around."

PRUNING

Early spring and late winter is the best time to prune many shrubs and small trees.

Shrubs that bloom in summer and autumn generally develop flowers on current seasons growth and should be pruned before the first flush of growth in the spring.

Shrubs that bloom in the spring or winter should be pruned immediately after flowering has finished.

In early summer, prune evergreens that are not in flower Prune conifers in late summer or early autumn. Prune other evergreens after flowering.

Pruning is practised to maintain plant health, control plant growth, and encourage flowering and fruiting. These objectives should be remembered as you prune.

Pruning should encourage plant health, not plant disease so it is important to prune properly using the correct pruning tools.

For twigs and light branches hand pruning shears or secateurs can be used.

Loppers may be used for branches up to 11/2(4cm) thick. Use a pruning saw for larger branches.

Hedge shears or clippers should be used to trim closely clipped hedges only.

All tools should be kept sharp. Sharp tools cut easier and avoid bruising the plant tissue. Bruising the plant causes slower healing of the wound and causes an increase in the probability of disease.

A clean cut should be made, the cut surface should have a smooth surface not a rough one that looks as if the tissue has been torn or pulled.

Care should be taken not to damage the plant around the cut, or rip or tear the bark above or below the cut. The cambium layer, a thin layer of cells just below the bark is important in wound healing and it is easily damaged.

"From tiny acorns mighty oaks grow"

PRUNING

Do not twist or turn the shears as you cut because you will damage the plant as well as the shears.

Unless a shrub is a topiary or part of a formal hedge it should not be closely clipped but allowed to develop naturally and pruned to keep in shape.

First remove all dead, diseased, or injured branches.

If necessary thin out the plant. Remove branches that cross each other or they will become entangled. If the shrub still looks too thick, remove some of the older branches.

Remove any branches that are distinctly different from the rest of the shrub. Cut back any very long growth to a bud.

To reduce the size of a shrub cut back each branch 4"-6"(10-15cm), to a new bud. Do not use hedge shears cut each branch separately.

Prune hybrid tea and Floribunda roses in March. Cut out dead, diseased or thin wood and trim back the main shoots. When cutting back main shoots count buds from base of each shoot and cut just above the second or third one. The length of shoot is less important than the number of buds.

Shrub roses are best pruned in winter. As both old and modern roses produce most of their flowers on shoots produced from old wood, prune lightly. Remove dead, thin and decayed wood and shorted main stems by one third.

Prune rambling roses in the autumn. Cut untidy, flowered shoots right down to the base and tie new shoots to the trellis or support. If there are a few new shoots, leave some of the flowered shoots in place cutting back just a little.

Climbing roses are also best pruned in the autumn. Remove any crossing or thin shoots and reduce the height of the main stems by about one third. This prevents them being blown about by the wind. Remove any side shoots that spoil the shape and cut back the others by about two thirds.

Miniature roses should be pruned in March. Cut off any dead, diseased or thin wood and trim back the main stems

"It will never rain roses. When we want to have more roses, we must plant more roses."

George Eliot

WATERING

For successful gardening it is important to know when and how to water.

There are no specific rules to follow, because when to water and how much to water depends on the kinds of plants, type of soil, time of year and the weather conditions.

Water only when plants need watering. The leaves of many plants will begin to curl in the early stages of a water shortage. Later, the leaves will become very limp and the plant is said to have "wilted". Plants should be watered before they wilt. Allowing them to wilt frequently will result in excessive leaf drop. Also, if plants are allowed to remain wilted for several days, they may never revive.

Some plants may not show symptoms of a water shortage until it is too late. These plants should be watered when the soil around them feels dry and crumbly.

New plantings will need special attention as when they were in containers in the nursery, water was applied daily.

During the first couple of seasons after being planted , new plants still have small root systems and can only absorb water from a limited soil area.

Check lawn grass for wilting - if the edges of the grass leaves start to curl and take on a dull bluish-grey colour, water the lawn immediately.

Lawns should be watered in the early morning, when winds and temperatures are low. Late morning, mid-day, and afternoon irrigation usually results in loss of water from evaporation.

When watering, give the soil a thorough soaking. Frequent, light sprinklings waste water and do not satisfy the water requirements of a plant growing in a hot, dry soil. It can also promote shallow root systems and these increase susceptibility to damage during dry spells.

*"Gardening requires lots of water - most of it in
the form of perspiration."*

Lou Erickson

WATERING

Water should be applied only as fast as the soil will absorb it. Watering with a hose nozzle turned on full force can do more damage than good. Fast-flowing water runs off quickly carrying soil with it and exposing plant roots to the sun. Sprinkler systems are more efficient.

Another method of watering is drip or trickle irrigation. Drip irrigation supplies plants with constant moisture at a low delivery rate through the use of low pressure plastic tubing installed on or below the ground surface.

Low pressure nozzles attached to plastic tubing release water at a slow rate into the soil around a plant. By wetting only the root area of the plant, there is a big saving in water, weeds are not encouraged to grow and plant growth is accelerated. This increased growth occurs because the plant is not subjected to wet and dry cycles that normally occur with other irrigation methods.

Garden plants should be watered most when they are maturing - flowers as the buds open, potatoes in flower, lettuces as they form a head etc.

Put a timer switch on sprinklers so they go on and off automatically and don't waste water.

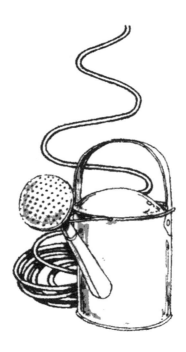

To a gardener there is nothing more exasperating
than a hose that just isn't long enough."

Cecil Roberts

WATER WISE TIPS IN A DROUGHT

Know your soil. Does it retain moisture or does it dry out quickly? Is the soil heavy in clay or rocks and gravel?

Plant the right plants for the right soils. If an area is often wet, plant thirsty plants there.

Use native plants in your landscape- they require less care and water than ornamental varieties.

Place plants in groups according to the amount of water they need.

If you have a slope, place lower-water-demand plants at higher elevations and those that need more water at lower elevations. The water from the higher areas will trickle down to the plants that demand more moisture

Prioritise watering - take care of new and young plantings, then more mature trees and shrubs.

Water in the early morning to take advantage of the cooler temperatures and reduce evaporation.

Water slowly, deeply and infrequently to avoid water runoff

Make sure the hose or sprinkler does not leak, and avoid placing watering devices where they waste water.

Help garden soils by using mulches, which dramatically reduce water evaporation from soils. Increase the mulch layers to 3"- 4"(7.5-10cm) thick.

When mulching, ensure trees, shrubs, and plants have a basin of mulch around them. During a drought the water tends to run off quickly and not soak down into the soil. Creating a basin around plants holds the water in until it has an opportunity to soak into the ground.

Don't fertilise or prune. Plants should not be encouraged to grow and both pruning and fertilising can encourage new growth. Fertilisers are salts, and without much water, the salts can build to harmful levels.

"You never miss the water till the well runs dry"

WATER WISE TIPS IN A DROUGHT

Remove any dead or weakened plant tissues to avoid secondary problems.

Control weeds. They compete with useful plants for water.

Shelter container plants by moving them to shady areas. This will reduce water loss due to evaporation.

Use a drip watering system. This can save up to 60% of the water used by sprinkler systems.

Raise your lawn mower cutting height- longer grass blades help shade each other, cut down on evaporation, and inhibit weed growth.

Consider letting the lawn go dormant, most lawn grasses will rebound when rains return.

Consider reducing your lawn and grassy areas in favour of more creative gardens, such as those that use more stone and drought-resistant perennial plants that have deeper root systems.

As a general rule, plants with grey or silvery foliage are the best drought-tolerant. They have fine hairs on their leaves that shade the leaf surface. Also consider using succulent plants (Yucca, etc.).

Use recycled water whenever you can. "Recycled water" includes rainwater collected from rooftops, cooking water, or any other water that has not been used for human or animal use.

"Irrigation of the land with seawater desalinated
by fusion power is ancient. It's called 'rain'."

Michael McClary

COMPOST

Compost is organic matter that has broken down. Grass clippings, potato peelings, onion tops and other vegetative waste material can be made into a valuable soil conditioner and used as plant food for garden beds in the autumn by remaining in a compost heap during the summer.

Compost can be used in several ways. It provides a good usable soil amendment for the garden and is less expensive than peat. Incorporated into the soil or around plants it is beneficial in improving soil texture, water holding capacity and nutrient retention. Compost can be used on the soil surface as mulch to control weeds and conserve moisture. Or, mix compost with sterilised soil and use it for potting plants.

Other materials such as leaves, waste from fresh summer vegetables, shredded paper or sawdust can be layered in to make excellent compost.

Old weeds can be added, but we only use weeds that haven't flowered otherwise you could add weed seed to the compost.

Do not add dog or cat manure as their worming treatment can also kill off composting worms.

Avoid adding meat and bones as they attract flies, rats and other vermin.

Do not include citrus peels as they are too acidic for worms.

Choose an out-of-the-way location for the compost area, since the heap may appear untidy. Choose a location that is convenient to the gardening area and to the kitchen door.

Decomposition of the plant matter will require heat and moisture for quick breakdown. The summer sun will provide the heat, but the heap must be soaked occasionally to give it moisture.

"You know you are a gardener, if you find compost a fascinating subject."

COMPOST

Animal manure is a rich, valuable garden soil additive and may be used between the layers of compost. The heat generated by the manure will induce quick decomposition of raw compost.

The compost should be turned with a garden fork from time to time to aerate and to promote even decomposition.

Cover the heap to keep excess rain from leaching out nutrients, keeping stray wildlife away and also helping to "heat up" the pile.

Save old tea bags and put one or two in the bottom of plant pots to help retain moisture. Also use teabags in the bottom of runner bean trenches.

Paper from an office shredder will rot well in a compost heap.

Make a 3ft(1m) cube with four posts and chicken wire as a leaf mould cage. Leaves rot more slowly than garden debris so it's best to rot them separately. Press the leaves down firmly to compress them - it takes about 18 months to have a rich mulch.

Always cover old potato tubers with other debris when they are put in the compost. This prevents any with blight fungus from sprouting and spreading spores that could infect a new season's crop.

Do not re-use old seedling compost as disease organisms may be present and the nutrients have been mostly used up.

Coffee grounds make an excellent mulch for plants that require acidic soil like blueberries, rhododendrons and roses.

Banana skins placed around rose bushes will rot down and provide nutrients

Getting water into peat-based potting mixes isn't easy. For small amounts, put the mix into a plastic bag, add water, and then knead the bag. For larger amounts, use a container such as a wheelbarrow, add the mix, then scoop out a centre hole and add warm (not cold) water, continually blending. Never add the mix to water; instead, always add water to the mix

A light sprinkling of fertiliser between layers of added compost will aid in decomposition and replace the nitrogen used in breaking down raw materials into compost.

"Compost - because a rind is a terrible thing to waste"

MULCHING

A layer of organic material several inches thick buffers the soil against compaction from the harsh effects of heavy rain and baking sun, and helps the soil retain oxygen so it can support vigorous plant roots. It improves any soil by blending valuable organic material, or humus, into its top layer as the mulch gradually decomposes.

A mulch helps conserve water by absorbing rainfall and preventing runoff. Soil covered by a layer of organic mulch stays damp much longer between rains or watering because the mulch blocks evaporation.

A good layer of organic mulch between newly planted groundcover plants discourages weeds during the time the plants need to grow larger, knit together, and cover the soil on their own.

Trees and shrubs thrive on mulch, too. Circles of organic material under them not only condition the soil and improve its fertility, but they also create a barrier to prevent injury to their trunks and stems from lawn mowers and string trimmers.

A layer of organic mulch on the bare soil in a garden shelters many kinds of beneficial organisms. Ground spiders and ants nest in rich organic material along the edges of lawns. These insects prey on pest insect larvae and eggs in the soil under the lawn and garden beds.

Avoid spreading mulch too thickly. A layer over 2"- 3" (5cm-7cm) can become a suffocating blanket blocking air and moisture from the soil. This causes plant roots to gravitate toward the soil surface in search of these essentials. In cases where surface tree roots are a problem, mulch lightly to improve the appearance of the yard, but don't try to bury the roots.

Organic mulch inevitably breaks down over time, and the mulch layer becomes thinner. Add mulch periodically, usually in the autumn.

Shredded paper is a suitable mulch for protecting soil and discouraging weeds. If it becomes unsightly when rains wet it down, cover it with a thin layer of leaves or bark nuggets.

"A fool looks for dung where the cow never browsed"

MULCH

During the winter, fluctuating temperatures alternately freeze and thaw the soil. This often disturbs plant roots and may leave bulbs or plants out of the soil. A winter mulch will not prevent soil from freezing, but it gives insulation to maintain more even low temperatures.

Add a mound of mulch to roses to prepare them for winter.

TYPES OF MULCH
Fallen leaves are a good mulch for bare soil in a garden.

Shred or chop them to stop them matting and block water from the soil.

Gravel is an appropriate mulch for arid landscapes and beds with plants that need good drainage, such as rock gardens.

Pine needles give a brown covering for the soil. Use them around acid-loving plants such as conifers, rhododendrons, and holly bushes.

Wood chips are long-lasting and inexpensive. Allow them to age for a few weeks, then spread them on paths and under trees and woody plants.

Leaf mould (partially decomposed leaves) contributes valuable organic matter to the soil as it decomposes. Use it for plants in woodland settings and informal gardens.

HOW TO MULCH A TREE
When mulching an established tree with grass growing beneath it, put a layer of cardboard over the lawn before spreading the mulch. This will keep the grass from penetrating the mulch.

Make the cardboard collar 2'- 3'(60-90cm) wide. Moisten to soften and easily conform to the contours of the ground and the root flare at the base of the trunk. Then cover it with wood chips.

Limit the mulch layer to 2"- 3" (5cm-7cm) so that the tree roots can still get sufficient air and moisture. Otherwise, they will migrate toward the soil surface. Be very careful not to pile mulch against the tree trunk. Unlike root bark, trunk bark can't handle constant moisture and will rot. If you wish, add a border of bricks, rocks, or other attractive material around the collar.

"He who plants a tree loves others besides himself"

GETTING RID
OF
GARDEN PESTS

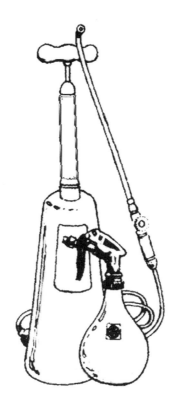

Many things love to come and live off your plants,
including bacteria, bugs, birds, and bunnies.
If you don't control them, entire crops can be ruined.
The result of your careful cultivation,
in your garden and in your life,
can be lost to predators in a short time.
Take a look at your life,
what toxic relationships, substances and emotions
are feeding on your energy
and taking away from what you have to give to others.
Eliminate them.

Vivian Elisabeth Glyck

GARDEN PESTS

ANTS

Ants are attracted by sweet foods and are generally harmless apart from the hills they make, but they can assist in the spreading of aphids from plant to plant.

Locate the ants' nest by sprinkling a little sugar and watch where the ants carry it.

If the nest cannot be found, identify where they are entering the house and the run they are using - they seem to use the same thin route. Place some proprietary ant powder or bait outside in this run. Make sure it is out of reach of children and pets.

Locate the ants' hill and sprinkle a liberal amount of talcum powder around and on it. The ants dislike talc and will move their colony several feet. Continue sprinkling the talc until the ants are moved to where you want them.

Boiling water poured into/onto the nest also works quite well.

Put some water in an empty jam jar, make sure there is some jam on the edge of the jar and this may tempt some of them for a swim.

Apparently ants never cross a chalk line so get out the chalk and draw a line wherever ants tend to march.

To deter ants, spray vinegar around doors, appliances and along other areas where they are located.

Dried cinnamon is a good ant deterrent and is very effective in places that chemicals cannot be used, eg. around ponds.

Ants hate peppermint. Mix some drops of oil with water in a sprayer and spray wherever there are ants. This is also really effective indoors.

To get rid of ants, mix a small bottle of clove oil in a large watering can with a rose sprinkler. Sprinkle this over the area where the ants are. First the flying ants leave the nest in droves then the soldier ants will follow them on foot.

"All good work is done the way ants do things:
Little by little. "

APHIDS

These are green-fly or black-fly which attack a wide range of outdoor or glasshouse plants, trees or shrubs.

Their colour varies from green, black or reddish to almost white or bluish.

The body is plump, semi-transparent, winged or wingless. They often exude a sticky honey dew on which a sooty mould grows.

All are sucking insects and may carry virus disease.

They usually attack the underside of the leaves or the tips of shoots but they can also attack the roots of some plants.

Early detection and action is essential. Leaf-curling, malformation and discoloration occurs soon after an attack.

A more-or-less organic way of controlling aphids is to make a garlic tea by crushing and then boiling a few bulbs. Allow to cool and then spray. Add a few drops of washing-up liquid to the mixture brew to assist adhesion.

Don't throw out old soap bars, melt them down in hot water and put them in a spray to use in the greenhouse. The result is an effective aphid-killer.

Proprietary sprays such as malathion, nicotine, derris or pyrethrum can be used making sure that the insects are covered. Systemic insecticides can also be used.

On fruit trees use a winter egg-killing spray.

Root infestations are best dealt with by pulling up the root stumps as soon as possible and burning them.

To get rid of greenfly on roses, in the spring crush a clove of garlic and bury it at the roots of the rose bush.

A simple way of removing greenfly and larvae from plants is to use strips of sticky tape. If placed lightly on a leaf or stem, it lifts the pests off without the tape sticking to the plant.

"Organic gardening is not just the avoidance of chemicals, in the larger view, it is organic living using nature's laws"

GARDEN PESTS

Hang old CD's around the garden to deter birds from attacking fruit during the daytime.

Bees are not harmful unless provoked, trapped or you are unfortunately in their line of flight.

If there is a swarm in your garden do not attempt to remove it yourself, Contact a local beekeeper or your local authority.

If you have bees in a chimney, light a fire in the grate and this should remove them safely and harmlessly. Some bumble bees are endangered species.

CATS

Save used teabags and dry them, add a few drops of Olbas oil, citronella oil or eucalyptus oil to each one and spread them around the areas in your garden frequented by cats.

Provide an area for them to use by turning over some dirt in a garden bed. Spray them with a hose or keep a spray bottle of water handy.

Sink a jam-jar of ammonia in the cat-path or save urine and spray onto area.

Place a small length of hose pipe in amongst your plants, cats and birds don't like snakes!

If using grated soap to deter cats it is best to use coal tar, or another tip is to sprinkle curry powder or chilli pepper powder around the boundaries where they frequent.

Scatter moth-balls on flowerbeds to deter cats from visiting your garden.

On gravel driveways scatter broken small pieces of orange peel around the borders to keep cats away.

To deter cats from using your borders as a convenience, place the trimmings from your pruned roses between the plants.

If there are rats or mice in a garden cats can do more good then harm!

"We are learning that success in horticulture and agriculture, depends on a good understanding of the birds"

EARWIGS

Earwigs feed at night and hide during the day under leaves or rubbish. Remove all debris that they can hide under.

Fill pots loosely with straw and set these up on canes or poles to entrap them. Shake the traps out daily over a bowl of paraffin or insecticide.

EELWORMS

There are different spices of eelworm. Each one keeps to its specific plant (including weeds) and even if its host is removed it can still remain in the soil in the form of a dormant cyst for three years or more.

The bulb and stem eelworm causes stunted growth in a wide rage of bulbous and herbaceous plants.

Leaf eelworms attack many flowering plants and one species is very destructive to chrysanthemums.

Root eelworms can attack many vegetables and flowering plants. One species of these can attack potato tubers resulting in little or no crop.

The root-knot eelworms attack a wide variety of plant hosts particularly cucumbers, tomatoes and flowers grown under glass.

There is no method of control that will eradicate the different species.

Reducing infestation or preventing it progressing is the best solution.

All weeds and rubbish must be removed, pots and seed boxes cleaned and sterilised, prepared seed and potting composts used and soil in greenhouse borders must be sterilised or replaced from a tested source.

All plants purchased should be from a reliable source.

Susceptible crops must not be planted in infested soil for

over 4 years. In a vegetable garden a long rotation should be strictly followed.

"Of all the living objects in gardens, the most easily transplantable is the gardener"

GARDEN PESTS

MICE
Use fruit and nut chocolate for bait instead of cheese.

Bait can be placed in a milk bottle or similar jar, which should be placed on a ramp (with the neck higher than the base). The mouse can then go in to feed but will not be able to get back out. The captured mouse can then be allowed to go free in a more suitable area (well away from the house).

Ensure any holes large enough to insert a ball pen in are filled, as mice can use these to enter the house.

When trying to catch mice, site traps horizontally around the edge of the room. This will then be effective whichever way the mouse runs.

If you don't know where the rodent is coming from, sprinkle flour on the floor around the area and it will then be evident from the footprints. A tray containing lard or solid fat can also do the trick.

If mice have destroyed a row of newly sown peas, the peas used in subsequent sowings should be coated in a mixture of paraffin and red lead made to a consistency of cream.

MILLEPEDES
These must not be confused with centipedes that are beneficial to the garden as they feed on various insects.

Millepedes have two pair of legs and curl up when disturbed.

Millipedes are from 1/2"-1"(1-2cm) long with a flat body. According to the species they can be black with white legs, yellowish-white to dull brown.

They feed on a variety of vegetable matter and often feed on tissue already damaged.

Eradication is virtually impossible but good general hygiene and cultivation keeps them at bay.

If there is a large infestation of millipedes they can be trapped by placing pieces of carrot or potato just under soil level. Check every few days and remove and destroy.

*"One of the worst mistakes you can make as a gardener
is to think you're in charge"*

Janet Gillespie

MOLES

If there is a problem with moles in the garden, find the run and place a small piece of gorse in the bottom. The prickles on the gorse will stop them returning. Alternatively, a child's "windmill" (the sort you get at the seaside) poked into the ground above the run causes vibrations that deters moles.

MOSQUITOES, GNATS AND MIDGES

Females feed on blood, biting mostly at dusk. Eggs are laid in stagnant water. Clean out guttering, bird baths, water butts etc. as these are ideal breeding sites.

Door and windows can be screened and repellents can be used on skin.

PEA MOTH

This small greyish-brown moth appears from mid-June to mid-August over the peas that are in flower or in pods. The caterpillars eat into the pods and cause damage.

Damage can be curtailed by sowing early and late crops and avoiding the mid-season. Regularly hoe between the rows to destroy the larvae.

RABBITS

The only secure method is to enclose the garden with 1"(2.5cm) mesh wire netting , 3'(1m) high and sunk 18"(50cm) below ground level.

A line of fish manure spread around the boundaries of the garden can act as a repellent but it must be renewed after heavy rain.

Pour vinegar into a wide-necked jar and soak corn cobs (cut in half) in it for five minutes, scatter around the vegetable or flower garden. Reuse the vinegar every two weeks.

Use red pepper, black pepper, cayenne or paprika as a dust to repel rabbits as they are always sniffing.

"All I need to know about life I learned from gardening."

GARDEN PESTS

Mix a well beaten egg, 1/2 tsp(2ml) Tabasco sauce and 1gall(5ltr) water. Paint on tree trunks to prevent munching. It will not harm the trees.

Make a solution of cow manure and water, spray on the garden.

SLUGS AND SNAILS

Bury empty shallow cans or empty grapefruit halves in the soil so that the top is level with the ground, fill the can or grapefruit with beer and the slugs crawl in, drink and die.

Bake egg shells in an oven to harden and then place around plants to prevent slugs damaging them. The slugs cannot get over the hardened shells. Or completely encircle the base of the plant with washed, roughly crushed eggshells. Ash and grit can also be effective.

Sprinkle slugs with salt to kill them.

Vaseline smeared around plant pots stops slugs getting to the plants inside.

Make a slug catcher by using a 1ltr plastic drink bottle. Cut the bottle two thirds of the way up all the way around, making two pieces. Cut around the neck of the bottle and discard the neck. Invert the section of bottle that is left to form a funnel inside the other part and staple together if necessary.

Put about 2"(5cm) of water into the bottle and a few slug pellets. This should be sunk in the flower bed so that the top is level with the soil. The idea is that the slugs and snails climb into the bottle, but as the slug pellets are contained within the bottle they are not harmful to birds and animals that come into the garden.

To prevent slugs and snails from attacking your plants, place a handful of bran in the bottom of a terracotta flowerpot and lay the pot on its side to distract them from your plants.

To deter slugs from crawling up into flower pots on a patio, wind some copper wire just under the rim (or a little lower) around the pot - it will give them a little electric shock.

"How pleasant the lives of the birds must be, living in love in a leafy tree."

Mary Howitt

WASPS

At their worst during August and September but die naturally by the end of autumn. Attracted by sweet food and drinks.

Stay still and they will soon go away. If you try to swat them this can cause their friends to come and help.

Trap with jars partly filled with water, jam and a drop of washing up liquid, covered with a punctured paper lid. Individual wasps can be destroyed by a proprietary wasp or fly killer.

Seek advice from environmental health department or pest control company before tackling wasp nests.

WEEVILS

These are a type of beetle with a snout-like head and legless.

They vary in colour, some with a sheen, stripes or bands and are mostly grey or brown to black about 1/2"(1.25cm) long.

Hiding by day and feeding at night they eat the tissues of many trees, bushes and plants.

The adults can be trapped in pieces of sacking or corrugated paper while the grubs may be picked off the roots of pot plants. The plants should be re-potted in fresh sterilised soil with an insecticide added.

WIREWORMS

These are slow-moving, shiny, yellowish-brown grubs common in most soils especially newly broken up turf.

They are larvae of the click beetles which are brown to black, 1/2"(1.25cm) long and click when disturbed. The larvae vary in length.

They feed on roots and stems of most plants and burrow into bulbs, potatoes and other root crops.

They do not affect the growth of established plants but seedlings or young plants may wilt and die. If there is a large infestation they can be trapped like the millepedes.

"The better the fruit, the more wasps to eat it."

German Proverb

INSECTICIDES

Before using any home-made spray, always pre-test on a small area of the plant to make sure it will not harm it.

To control aphids - Chop up a few garlic gloves, one large onion, a few chive leaves and place in a blender. Fill the blender half full with water. After blending the ingredients well, strain to form a clear solution and discard the pulp. Add additional water to make 1gall(5ltr) of spray. When using on plants, make sure to spray the undersides of the leaves where the aphids hide. This spray will kill the aphids but not harm other beneficial insects. It also helps to control white-flies.

For organic insecticide spray, boil a whole bulb of chopped garlic until it's soft. Put it into 1gall(5ltr) water and add 1 tablespoon of biodegradable detergent. Leave for a day, strain and use as required.

Garlic Spray for wire-worm, slugs, caterpillars and weevils. Chop 3oz(75g) garlic and mix with 2tsp mineral oil. Leave for 24 hours, add 1pt(500ml) water with 2tsp dissolved soap added. Stir well and strain into a plastic container. To use, dissolve one part of the mixture with twenty parts of water and spray on to the leaves of affected vegetables and the surrounding soil.

Insect Repellent Spray - Mix together garlic, onion, lavender leaves or flowers, yarrow and mint with just enough water to mix. Leave standing at room temperatures for 24 hours in a closed container. Strain and add a few drops of detergent to help its ability to stick to the plants. Then add equal quantity of water and spray as required.

Rhubarb Aphids Spray - Chop 6-7 green leaves of rhubarb and boil in 4pt(2ltr)of water for 30 minutes. Strain and cool. Add a few flakes of soft soap and use as required.

Tobacco Spray for aphids, bugs and small caterpillars - Take 5g of tobacco (approx. 1-2 large pinches) and pour over about 2pt(1ltr) of boiling water and let boil for 15 minutes or until the brew looks the strength of weak tea. Let it cool and strain. It is best to use this fresh but it can be kept for a few days.

"There is nothing in a caterpillar that tells you it's going to be a butterfly."

Repellent for cucumber beetles - mix a hand full of wood ash with a handful of Hydrated Lime and 2gall(10ltr) water. Mix well, then with a hand spray bottle, spray both sides of your cucumber leaves.

To get rid of powdery mildew from cucumber or strawberry plants, mix _ oz(6g) baking soda (bicarbonate of soda) with 1gall(5ltr) water. Using a spray bottle, spray on leaves weekly to rid the plants of the mildew.

Instead of using chemicals on mildewed plants, make a solution of 90% water and 10% fresh milk and spray it on to the plant. Enzymes in the milk will attack the mildew. Don't go over 30% milk or you may end up with foul-smelling plants.

Spray milk on apples and lettuce to control mildew. For large areas, dilute one part milk in nine parts water.

To kill weeds without using harmful chemicals, fill a spray bottle with vinegar and zap the weeds with it - just make sure not to spray your nearby crops. This will work on weed seedlings as well as full grown plants. For particularly tough weeds, use cider vinegar, which has a higher acidity.

To help weed easily between slabs or crazy paving, pour on the slightly salted boiling water after cooking potatoes. Even dandelions soon go after a couple of treatments.

To rid roses of black spot disease, mix 1tbsp bread soda, 1tbsp vegetable oil and 1tbsp washing-up liquid in 1gall(5ltr) water and spray on the roses once a week.

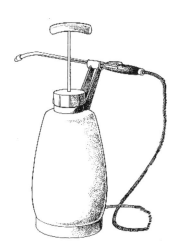

"A good gardener always plants three seeds -
one for the bugs, one for the weather and one for himself."

Leo Aikman

WEED CONTROL

Although it is best to prevent weeds seeds from germinating or becoming established in the garden sometimes it will be necessary to deal with them.

Use opaque plastic sheeting to warm the soil for heat-loving tomatoes, peppers and strawberries. The plastic absorbs heat during the day and keeps the soil warm at night. This is especially helpful during cool spring weather.

The plastic also smothers the weeds between the rows and reduces evaporation from the soil beneath.

Thick black plastic sheets can be used and these can usually be reused the following season.

Before planting peppers, tomatoes or strawberries, lay the plastic on the ground where the plants will grow. Cut 6"(15cm) holes in the plastic every 2'(50cm). Dig a hole for each transplant where there is a hole in the plastic, add organic matter and plant. Be sure there is enough plastic on all sides to fully cover a mature root system.

If using drip irrigation in the garden, put the drip lines under the plastic. If using sprinklers, dampen the soil before laying down the plastic and cut the holes larger to ensure that enough moisture enters the ground from the sprinklers.

After everything is planted, weigh down the edges of the plastic with rocks or few mounds of soil.

Throughout the summer, the plastic will help control weeds, reduce moisture loss, and help to ripen warm-weather fruits and vegetables. By leaving the plastic in place over the winter, the soil will be weed-free and easy to work come planting time in the next spring. Note that the plastic gives slugs and snails a place to hide.

Regular hoeing and hand weeding can control most weeds. Hoeing is a very effective method of dealing with annual weeds. Hoe as soon as you see the weeds surfacing above the soil. Push the hoe just below the soil level to sever the weeds. Try to hoe when the ground is dry so weed seeds brought to the surface will not germinate.

"A man of words and not deeds,
Is like a garden full of weeds."

There are garden tools now available that are specially made for removing weeds. Choose one that removes the greatest amount of root system and the least amount of surrounding soil.

Perennial weeds are best dug up, as they are difficult to control by other methods. Perennial weeds tend to spread by their creeping stems or roots and fragments of root. Ensure that all the roots are dug up or they will return.

Planting ground covering plants will cut down the amount of weeding. However before planting, all perennial weeds need to be removed. Having ground cover doesn't mean you will always have a weed free area, but it will be easier to maintain.

Mulching can suppress annual weeds and conserve soil moisture. Perennial weeds will still come through the mulch, so need to be dug out by the roots. Use well rotted compost and grass cuttings, providing the lawn they came from is weed free or use de-composed wood chipping.

To help prevent the spread of disease, destroy diseased plants. Try to remove infected plants as soon as you notice them. Otherwise, the disease might spread to nearby plants. It usually is easier to spot disease problems in trees and shrubs in the summer or autumn when leaves are present. Avoid composting diseased plants, including fallen leaves from diseased trees or shrubs, since several disease-causing organisms can survive in compost.

When removing diseased branches, prune 2"-3"(5-7cm) below the infected area. If you do cut into the infected part of the limb, sterilise your pruning equipment by wiping the blades with rubbing alcohol or a mixture of one part household bleach and nine parts water.

Clean and prepare garden beds in winter to have them ready for the spring. Dig in, compost, or remove and destroy crop refuse soon after you finish harvesting your garden.

Removing plant refuse eliminates places where disease-causing organisms can over-winter.

"What is a weed?
A plant whose virtues have not yet been discovered. "

Ralph Waldo Emerson

WEED CONTROL

When using chemical weed-killer always carefully read the instructions on the product to ensure that you have the correct product for the task.

Never store garden chemicals outdoors. Place large bags on a rack to allow air to circulate beneath.

Never mix two different types of garden chemicals unless the manufacturers specifically state on the instructions that this can be done.

Do not spray any garden chemical on a windy day or in frosty weather.

Adjust the nozzle on the garden sprayer so that the spray is just a fine mist.

Always clearly mark any watering cans or sprayers used for weed-killer. Do not use these for watering or for applying other garden chemicals.

Contact-acting insecticides and fungicides only work if they make contact with the organisms. Systemic-acting types are taken up into the sap and spread throughout the plant.

If a lawn is treated with weed-killer the grass cuttings should not be put in the compost for six months.

"Man is by definition the first and primary weed under whose influence all other weeds have evolved."

Jack R. Harland

GARDEN TOOLS

The gardener does not love to talk,
He makes me keep the gravel walk;
And when he puts his tools away,
He locks the door and takes the key.

Away behind the currant row
Where no one else but cook may go,
Far in the plots, I see him dig,
Old and serious, brown and big.

Robert Louis Stevenson

Garden Tips

If plastic garden furniture is stained, make a paste of baking soda and water, apply it for a few minutes then wipe off.

To preserve aluminium garden furniture and metal tools over the winter apply oil (either cooking oil or motor oil). Wipe off before using again though.

Paint the handles of gardening tools with leftover paint - the brighter the better, to make them easier seen in the garden.

Clay soil can be difficult to dig, sharpen the end of the spade with a file to make it easier.

Use an old bum-bag to keep secateurs, plant labels, string, penknife and other garden tools nearby. The expanding waist strap will enable it to go comfortably over bulky jackets and jumpers.

Wrap a long length of string to one handle of secateurs and a few elastic bands to the other handle, they always comes in handy in the garden.

Keep an old oily rag in the garden shed for wiping tools after use, especially at damp times of the year - it will help keep them rust-free and clean.

To avoid getting kinks in a garden hose, coil in a figure 8 not a circle.

An old wheel rim makes an ideal storage place for a garden hose when not in use. Hang on a garage or shed wall.

If the handles of tools, mowers or shears are uncomfortable to hold, buy a foam bicycle handlebar grip. Slip the grips over the tool handles, using washing up liquid or Vaseline if it proves difficult. Or slit the grip and slip it over the handle. Pipe insulating foam could also be used.

If the hose springs a leak, make a temporary repair by inserting a cocktail stick into the hole. Snap the stick off as close to the hose as possible and wrap around with insulating tape or waterproof tape. This should extend by about 5cm(2") each side of the hole. As the wood absorbs the water it will expand and seal the hole.

"Coiled like a garden hose neatly put away."

TOOLS

Always buy strong, good quality tools and look after them well. If you can afford it buy stainless steel as they will last a lifetime and are easier to clean.

When choosing tools handle them before buying to make sure they feel good in your hand and try out for balance and weigh. With shovels and spades, check the length of the handle for comfort.

SHOVELS: Round-pointed shovels are strictly for digging. The long-handled version works well for light-duty, stand up digging, while a short-handled shovel is better for deep digging. A flat-ended shovel doesn't work well for digging, but it's perfect for things like scooping compost and for cutting borders. Half-moon shovels or spades work well for keeping borders tidy and straight.

RAKES: A wider-than-usual grading rake with teeth made from nearly indestructible nylon is ideal for levelling newly prepared ground or for drawing down the length of raised beds. Rakes with metal tines tend to last longest. They also can make the job easier because the teeth don't bend when they hit a heavy patch of leaves.

PITCHFORKS: Square-tine versions are much stronger and can take a good deal of punishment. Use a pitchfork to loosen the subsoil in beds by simply driving it into the soil and gently rocking back and forth.

PRUNING SHEARS OR SHARP SECATEURS: A good pair of hand clippers used for trimming rose bushes and shrubs.

LOPPERS: This long-handled cutting tool is versatile enough to use for trimming rose bushes or cutting through branches about 1"(2.5cm) in diameter. Useful in areas hard to reach with clippers or small shears.

HEDGE SHEARS: Long-handled, flat-bladed hedge shears designed to cut evenly across a plane, either horizontal or vertical. Unless you have a large amount of greenery, hand hedge sheers will work just as well as electric shears.

"You can bury a lot of troubles digging in the earth."

TOOLS

TANK SPRAYER: Very useful for pest or weed control or for fertilising an area. There are 1gall(5ltr) sprayers for smaller yards, and wheeled multi-gallon sprayers for larger areas.

GARDEN HOSE: The length should be determined by the size of the garden. Too long a hose will become a tangled mess while too short a hose is a nuisance. A rack or reel to keep the hose in good shape helps eliminate kinks that can impede flow already compromised by low water pressure in some areas and to make storage convenient when the hose isn't in use. A more expensive hose usually is better able to survive a hot summer and freezing winter temperatures. Check if the hose is made from material that is safe for drinking water.

WHEELBARROW: A wheelbarrow can be used for a variety of gardening activities from moving dirt for a new plant bed to mixing concrete for a patio fix. If all you plan to do is move leaves, plastic wheelbarrows weigh less.

SPREADER: These help to spread fertiliser more evenly over the garden.

A SQUARE-ENDED SPADE for digging large holes and double-digging.

A HOE for weeding, cultivating, and opening seed furrows.

A TROWEL (or a large kitchen spoon) for transplanting and applying dry fertilisers.

A WATERING CAN and maybe a sprinkler system.

A FILE, sharpening stone, or diamond file to keep tools sharp.

OTHERS: A pruning saw, lawn mower, cotton gloves and hat.

Wipe tools with an oily rag before putting them away to keep them in good order for next time.

Keep hand shears in a sturdy leather sheath that easily fits on a belt. This will not only keep them handy, but it will prevent them from poking holes through pockets.

"Tickle the earth with a hoe, it will laugh a harvest."

SHARPENING GARDEN TOOLS

Since gardening tools are expensive it pays to take care of them properly. The best way to ensure that your tools will last a long time is to give them a thorough once-over before you put them away for the winter.

Keep a small garden trowel working smoothly by regularly sharpening the edge with a file.

Shovels, trowels, hoes, pruning shears and hedge clippers will all work better if sharpened regularly.

Before starting, clean all rust off the tools to be sharpened.

Always wear safety goggles and leather gloves when filing or sharpening metal.

Cut up some sandpaper to sharpen pruning shears. Use a 320-grit wet or dry sandpaper, and cut three to four strips of sandpaper. Do this once a week for shears that are used frequently, and put a drop of lubricant on the pivot screw to keep the shears working smoothly. This method also works for sharpening scissors.

On a hedge clipper, first clean the blades with a piece of steel wool and make sure none of the blades are bent. If a blade is bent, loosen the pivot nut and separate the blades, put the bent blade in a vice and tweak it until it is straight.

Once the blades are straight, clamp one blade in the vice with the blade side facing up. Examine the factory edge, hold the file with both hands and follow the direction of the bevel. Move the file in one broad stroke, moving away, along the entire cutting area. Apply moderate pressure on the downward side of the coarse, metal file, going across the blade. Repeat this motion several times until the whole edge shows an even line of exposed, clean metal. This can take up to 10 strokes. Repeat the process on the other blade.

Remove burrs from the blade by placing a sheet of 300-grit wet or dry sandpaper on a smooth flat piece of plywood. Lightly sand the backside of the blade using a circular motion. After several circles, check to see if the burrs are gone. Re-assemble the hedge clippers and cut away.

"Nothing is particularly hard if you divide it into small jobs".

SHARPENING GARDEN TOOLS

Use a file to remove nicks and smooth the edges of shovels and trowels. Before beginning, clean the trowel or shovel thoroughly with steel wool. Coat with a silicone spray for a finishing touch. This prevents rust and keeps soil from sticking to the tool.

Sharpen a garden hoe by filing the inside edge first, working away from the handle. Then take the feathered edge off the outside surface. A sharp hoe cuts through the ground with ease.

Clean all metal surfaces to remove any dirt that can harbour moisture and cause the metal to rust. Small and large stiff wire brushes work best for this task.

Once all the dirt has been removed, soak a cloth in motor oil, WD-40 or vegetable oil and coat the metal surfaces thoroughly. The oil coating will prevent rust from forming on the metal should moisture find its way into your garage or tool shed.

Wooden tool handles should be treated to prevent drying and cracking that can lead to splinters. Soak a rag in boiled linseed oil and rub the handle, allowing it to absorb the oil. Check to see that any screws or bolts are fastened securely.

Clean resinous sap from the metal surfaces of loppers or secateurs/pruners with a cloth soaked in methalyted spirit, turpentine or warm soapy water, then file the cutting edge.

Oil pivot points with a light household oil or WD-40. A honing stone should be used to sharpen these tools, but the technique is difficult so it is better to get an authorised service agent to sharpen high quality shears or secateurs.

Clean your gardening tools throughout the growing season, rather than waiting until the end of the year to do it. Get a good size barrel or bucket, fill it with sand and add a quart of motor oil, then each time you use your tool, stab it a few times in the sand. The grit of the sand will knock the dirt off the metal surfaces and the oil will put a nice shine on the tool and keep it from rusting.

A regular garden hose pumps out 20 gallons of water per minute. If left on for 24 hours, that's 28,800 gallons... Better not forget to turn it off!

"He that would perfect his work must first sharpen his tools".

LAWNMOWERS

Before putting your lawnmower away for the winter, give it a thorough cleaning and check up.

Disconnect electric cables from sockets or spark plugs and battery cable on a petrol filled mower and remove caked-on grass and mud from around the blades.

To prevent rusting when not in use, wipe all moving parts with a lightly oiled rag.

Lubricate all moving parts; spray rust inhibitor on the blade and other unpainted metal parts.

Check if the blades and cutters need sharpening, tightening or even replacing.

Examine electric mower cables and any with signs of damage or badly worn should be replaced immediately.

If you have a motor mower, drain the petrol and oil tanks and clean the spark plug. Fill oil tank with clean oil but leave the petrol tank empty as petrol deteriorates.

Get replacement parts or repairs done before storing for the winter as it is more difficult to get them done in the springtime.

Lightly sand and paint any rusted or peeling spots on the mower's metal body.

Never leave a motor mower standing for months on a damp surface or in a damp place as this will inevitably make it difficult to start in Spring. Stand it on a piece of cardboard or a block of wood and keep the area as well ventilated as possible to avoid condensation.

If the mower refuses to start, take out the plug and dip the sparking end in petrol, replace, connect and the mower should start.

"Lawnmower: a magic wand for making teenagers disappear."

Michael Garofalo

SAFETY TIPS WHEN USING LAWNMOWERS

Fill a petrol-fuelled mower outdoors and keep away from cigarettes or other heat sources. Wipe up any spills and replace petrol cap immediately, securing tightly.

Do not turn petrol mower on its side to inspect underneath which will result in the petrol and/or oil leaking out.

If blades of a lawnmower need examined or get clogged with wet grass, switch off the engine and disconnect the spark plug before examining the blades or removing the grass.

Make sure that electric mowers are fitted with a circuit breaker. This will prevent any nasty accident should it come into contact with moisture or the cable is damaged in any way.

Cables should run behind electric lawnmowers, never cut towards a flex, or use it in wet conditions.

Never clean or adjust electrical gardening equipment while they are still plugged in, make sure they are switched off first.

Never wash electrical gardening equipment with water.

Before mowing, clear the lawn of any debris as this can be picked up and spun out by the blades causing accidents.

Never run mower over gravel.

Wear heavy shoes or boots when mowing. Avoid loose clothing, jewellery and sandals. Tie long hair back.

Mow across a slope rather than up and down. You will have better control of the mower and will be less likely to fall towards the mower.

Turn the engine off when leaving it unattended, however quick you intend to be. Never allow children to use a lawnmower.

"The grass may be greener on the other side of the fence, but you still have to mow it."

HEALTHY GARDENING

*If you grow a garden
you are going to shed some sweat,
and you are going to spend some time bent over;
you will experience some aches and pains.
But it is in the willingness
to accept this discomfort
that we strike the most telling
blow against the power plants
and what they represent.*

GARDEN TIPS

If you hate wearing gardening gloves, rub petroleum jelly into the hands and push it well under the fingernails before gardening and this makes hand cleaning much easier. Or scrape nails over a bar of soap and they will be easier cleaned.

To clean hands after gardening put a little olive oil and a little sugar on the hands and rub well into the skin. Remove with warm soapy water.

To remove a splinter from your finger, put a little damp sugar over the affected area and cover with a piece of sticking plaster. After a few days the skin will have softened and the splinter can be easily forced to the surface.

Always wear gloves when handling bone-meal especially if you have cuts on you hands.

The sap of the poinsettia is an irritant - always remember to wash hands after handling

Rub Vanilla Extract on skin to repel gnats.

Always wear goggles when using hedge trimmers, strimmers, chainsaws or garden shredders.

Only store garden chemicals in their original packaging. Keep in a secure place out of reach of children or animals.

GARDENING WARM-UPS
These stretches prepare for the lifts, bends, and pulls common to working in the garden.

Upper Body Twist - Stand with hands on hips. Slowly turn upper body as far as possible to the left for a count of 5. Turn to the right for a count of 5. Repeat 10 times.

Upper Body Stretch - Stand with back straight and arms at your sides. Stretch arms straight out in front of you and hold for a count of 5. Return arms to sides. Repeat 10 times.

Now, stretch arms back until shoulder blades touch. Hold for a count of 5. Return arms to sides. Repeat 10 times

*"Callused palms and dirty fingernails precede
a green thumb."*

HEALTHY GARDENING

Gardening is a popular leisure activity for many people, however it can be difficult if a person has health conditions that limit movement or stamina. Even among fit people awareness is growing that gardening can take a greater physical toll than necessary. The solution lies in garden planning and layout, lifting, and ergonomic tools, adapting the work or tool to the individual rather than vice versa.

PLANNING
Be aware of your own physical limitations Plan your tasks and organise the tools you will need before you start. Break the task down and take rest breaks.

Before going into the garden take an extra ten minutes to warm up the muscles with stretches and warm up exercises

Lifting with your legs, not your back, can help prevent injury.

It is important to position yourself so that muscles can be used for maximum efficiency. Maintaining an upright posture rather than continually reaching forward is a safer and more efficient use of muscles.

Joints shouldn't be locked when standing. Sitting in a squatting position can be hard on the joints and difficult to get up from.

Regarding arms, the straighter the elbow and the farther away it is from the body, the less efficient the position.

Change position and tasks frequently and don't spend hours pruning or digging.

SENSIBLE GARDEN PLANNING
Start with a small garden area that can be managed without excess exertion. It should be located near the house and the water supply to reduce hauling long lengths of hose.

If possible, the garden area, tool storage and work surfaces and watering sources should be close together.

Consider putting in extra garden seating.

*"Gardening begins with daybreak
and ends with backache"*

HEALTHY GARDENING

Paths should be placed in the most direct route. Narrow pathways, steps and uneven paved surfaces can create dangerous and inconvenient access problems.

Gravel paths require constant maintenance and can be difficult and dangerous to walk on. Non-slip, hard, flat paving can be used without detracting from the appearance of the garden.

Make garden paths wide enough so that all the heavy stuff can be hauled by a four-wheeled cart or a wheelbarrow instead of by you.

Incorporate some back-friendly principles into your garden design. Raised beds and trellises are easier to maintain than in-ground beds.

Limit bed depth to no more than twice the distance you can reach without straining.

To reduce water hauling, set up a rain barrel or hose near the garden, water weighs more than 8lb(4kg) per gallon. Or install an automated drip or soaker hose watering system.

SMART DIGGING AND LIFTING
Keep your back straight when digging. When ready to plunge your shovel into the soil, remember that your spine is weaker if it's twisted, so face your shovel as you work and avoid digging in such a way that your back could be jerked to one side.

The way you use your shovel makes a difference to your back. Keep the blade vertical as you insert it into the soil for better leverage when you pull back on the handle.

If you have to lift, reduce the load. It is better to lift a shovel more times with less soil than fewer times with a heavy load each time. As well, you'll get more aerobic benefit and less back strain.

Buying garden products in extra-large bags may mean savings in the pocket but not for the back. Even lifting 25lb(10kg) pounds can cause injury, especially if you hold the bag low or far out in front. Choose bags with handles if possible, and lift with bent knees and straight back.

"Gardening: a leisure activity of little leisure and much activity."

Rather than moving the whole bag, divide it into smaller, more manageable loads.

Set heavy objects that you'll need to lift again on a table instead of the ground. Use a garden cart or trolley to move heavy bags and containers around.

To drag a heavy bag for a short distance, face it with bent knees and straight back and pull it while straightening your legs.

FRIENDLY TOOLS

As you work, keep your wrist as close as possible to its neutral position, that is the position it's in when you're not using your hand. If your wrist is bent in any other direction, you have less strength and are more prone to injury.

A wrist support in the form of a splint or brace prevents the wrist from bending without inhibiting finger movement.

Wider handles 11/2"(3.5cm) in diameter reduce hand strain. Similarly, cushion textured grips require less effort to hold, and reduce or eliminate blisters. Wrap your thumb around the tool handle to avoid the strain of positioning it along the handle.

It is important to vary your hand motions, take frequent rests, and stop at the first sign of pain.

There are a large selection of ergonomically designed garden tools now available so choose well-designed tools and learn the best position for a tool-task combination.

When it comes to long-handled tools, the longer the handle, the better (when you're standing). The less you bend, the less chance of back strain or injury. Long-handled tools with bent handles allow you to work without bending.

Slip pistol-grip handles or spongy tubes onto the end of the handles of rakes, hoes, and hand tools to make them more comfortable for hands and backs.

"A razor may be sharper than an axe,
but it cannot cut wood. "

HEALTHY GARDENING

Whenever possible, keep a stool or small folding chair in the garden to rest on or to sit down while working. A garden kneeler has a kneeling pad and side handles for getting up and down. It can be turned upside down for use as a stool.

If you must kneel, use cushioned strap-on knee pads or pants with padded knees.

Use the ball of your foot, not the instep to push a spade into the ground. Wear leather boots rather than wellingtons when digging.

Make your own planting devices. Polyvinyl (PVC) pipe, 2"-3(5-7cm) in diameter can be cut to 3'-4'(1-11/2m) in length, depending on how tall the user is. Sharpen one end so it can be used to draw a furrow in soil prepared for planting. Drop seeds at regular intervals through the pipe to provide the seed spacing. Turn over the pipe and drag it over the soil to fill the furrow.

Grow crops that can be managed without stooping as much. For example, small fruits such as blueberries, raspberries, vines, roses and other perennials can often be cared for without stooping all the way over.

Avoid numerous trips. Make carrying easier with a sturdy box or basket with a handle to collect and hold seeds, plants and tools etc.

Combination tool systems are available with interchangeable tool heads and handles of varying lengths and weights. Some tools are designed for more than one action or use, which reduces the number of tools you need to carry around.

Lawn mowers can be heavy and difficult to use. Mowers with an electric starter cause less frustration and are easier on your back. A self-propelling mower will help to prevent back strain. Electric mowers suit some people, but need to be operated methodically to avoid problems with the power cord and some users may find the swinging motion difficult to manage. Battery operated mowers tend to create less noise and vibration.

"Have patience. All things change in due time.
Wishing cannot bring autumn glory
or cause winter to cease."

Ginaly-li

HEALTHY GARDENING

Wheelbarrows are useful for gathering rubbish or moving heavy items around the garden. Wheelbarrows with two wheels rather than one are usually easier to use and the load is taken over the wheels rather than through the handles.

HOW TO AVOID OTHER DANGERS

Always secure a ladder to a branch or other support if using it to cut a high hedge.

Do not over-stretch when doing work in a garden pond. Lay large planks or a strong ladder across the pond and work from these.

Only use chemicals specifically sold for use in a garden. Do not use farm chemicals as they require special handling and application procedures.

Laburnum and Yew leaves can be poisonous to eat so it is advisable not to plant these in a garden where there are young children.

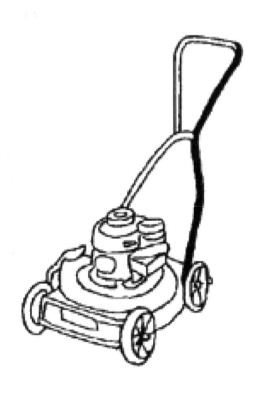

"Gardening gives me fun and health and knowledge.
It gives me laughter and colour.
It gives me pictures of almost incredible beauty."

John F. Kenyon

117

Garden Hints

When planting peas and beans, the rows should always run north and south. This makes sense since the sun moves from east to west and gives the plants maximum sunshine.

When planting your tomatoes, place 2 crumbled egg-shells in the bottom of each hole. This is an excellent source of calcium (an insufficient amount of calcium can cause blossom end rot). Also use crumbled egg-shells around the base of plants to protect them from cut worms.

Store ginger root in the soil of a potted basil plant. The ginger helps the basil plant flourish.

To harvest and cure onions properly, wait until 75% of the tops have fallen over naturally before harvesting the crop. Store them in a dry, shady place with good ventilation, such as an outdoor shed or barn, for 10 days to two weeks. After the onions have cured, put them in slatted crates or mesh bags. Store them indoors in a cellar with low humidity and temperatures between 33oF/3oC and 45oF/7oC.

Put 1-2 tbsp Epsom Salts in the hole before placing the tomato plant. Then cover with soil and water as usual.

The use of Epsom Salt is thought to add magnesium to the soil and help prevent blossom end rot. Generally, tomatoes tend to be heavy users of magnesium.

Before filling a strawberry barrel with compost, stand a piece of drainpipe or cardboard tube upright in the centre and fill with pebbles. As you fill with compost gradually remove the tube releasing the pebbles. This will act as a central drainage system preventing the soil from becoming waterlogged.

Sow seeds when it's dry; set plants when it's wet. If soil stays in a moist ball when squeezed hard, it is still too wet to plant seeds. Wait until the soil crumbles.

Weed after a rainfall as weeds pull easier. If you need to weed and it hasn't rained, water your garden first.

"The love of gardening is a seed once sown that never dies."

Gertrude Jekyll